Walter Ochanda

The Trials of Jonam

Trials of Jonam

JustFiction Edition

Imprint

Any brand names and product names mentioned in this book are subject to trademark, brand or patent protection and are trademarks or registered trademarks of their respective holders. The use of brand names, product names, common names, trade names, product descriptions etc. even without a particular marking in this work is in no way to be construed to mean that such names may be regarded as unrestricted in respect of trademark and brand protection legislation and could thus be used by anyone.

Cover image: www.ingimage.com

Publisher:
JustFiction! Edition
is a trademark of
Dodo Books Indian Ocean Ltd. and OmniScriptum S.R.L publishing group

120 High Road, East Finchley, London, N2 9ED, United Kingdom
Str. Armeneasca 28/1, office 1, Chisinau MD-2012, Republic of Moldova, Europe
Printed at: see last page
ISBN: 978-613-9-42565-5

THE TRIALS OF JONAM

WALTER OCHANDA

THE

TRIALS

OF

JONAM

THE

TRIALS OF JONAM

A Play of Three Acts

By
Walter Ochanda

PREFACE

A bit of Wadelai history which is the background to this play is pretty well known. Wadelai in whose name the village was named after was charismatic and respectable leader of the Jonam people. His chiefdom had a strong relationship with the Kingdom of Bunyoro.

Against him stood the arrival of Major General E.R Owen who was mandated to establish a command center and the British government administration in Wadelai. Wadelai became weary and pale. The defeat of King Kabalega troubled chief Wadelai.

In 1894, Major General Owen arrived and the British flag was hoisted at Wadelai on both banks of the river Nile. With Maj. Gen. Owen, was also Mr. Edward who issued administrative directives. These directives had two main provisions. First, a promise of protection, supply of goods and services and the transition of Wadelai to Town. Second and most important was unhindered access to Wadelai's vast land, forest, wild game (elephants, Rhinos) and labour force. The one sided lecture ended at 3:30PM without a single reply from Chief Wadelai.

In the years that followed, the officials from the Empire on which the Sun never set subjected the Jonam people to forced labour and exploitation. The industrial revolution had turned its heads on Africans, including the Jonam people. The officials were under strict order to supply raw materials for their industries. Since the Jonam economy was organized in such a way that it could not provide steady supply of the required raw materials.

The situation required the quest for direct take-over and control of the land, economy and administration of the Jonam enclaves and sub-chiefdoms. For instance, if the center needed cotton for cloth and soap industry, the Jonam were compelled to concentrate on the production of these commodities in commercial quantities so that their industries could have adequate and steady supply of these products.

The main justification for the full control and take-over was to ensure that the Jonam would produce demanded produce rather than food crops which were on demand in the local economy. Therefore, the colonial administration had to enforce direct control of the Jonam land, economy and political administration in order to farm the type of produce demanded by their industries and people back in Europe.

Mr. Edward maintained direct control and effective occupation of the Jonam through forced labour. The Jonam were forced to work in the colonial plantations and hunting undertakings. This was because the Jonam were not familiar to the colonial economy and system of production. They had to be forced to work on the cotton fields.

To force the Jonam to work in the cotton plantations, logging sites, Mr. Edward and his cohorts employed a number of strategies to force them to comply or make their labour force available. First, they started to take of Jonam use of occupancy whatever land they wanted by providing flimsy reasons such as the area is gazzetted for development projects or training facility, and they simultaneously assembled Jonam labour to tilt the land or to farm it for cotton, or groundnuts for oil.

In instances where Jonam people were reluctant to deprive themselves of their land and were unwilling to work for Mr. Edward, such land as the colonial administration wanted would be confiscated and the Jonam labour compelled. The means of doing this was by creating proxy sub-chiefs like Coope who were willing to enforce legal measures design expressly to compel the Jonam natives to apply for land grabbed from them, to occupy the same land, under the condition that they will work for Mr. Edward for a reward. Subsequently, ambitious men like Coope became colonial agents.

When lands formerly occupied by Jonam people are confiscated, or otherwise grabbed for colonial projects, the creation of a labour supply out of the displaced Jonam people was readily available because the people would then be asked if they were willing to live on the land and make means of surviving from tilling and working on the same land for the colonial administrators.

Since, they had been displaced of their land, the Jonam had no choice and means of livelihood other than to work for Mr. Edward unwillingly. They were forced to work for Mr. Edward because they must survive together with their families and relatives. The proceeds from the cotton plantations, logging, elephant tusks and Rhino tusks, ground nuts, sim - sim and others were regularly loaded on a ferry docked on the bank of the river Nile at Wadelai.

After nearly half a Century of force labour, exploitation and suffering, Chief Wadelai died. His son Jonam was inaugurated as the new Chief of Wadelai. The next morning, he arranged for a meeting with Mr. Edward. During the meeting, Chief Jonam registered his frustration and voiced the complains of his natives against forceful land eviction, indiscriminate hunting, logging, forced labour and torture of his subjects. He also demanded an immediate release of all detainees without preconditions.

Chief Jonam's demands fell on deaf ears, as new punitive measures were introduced, including movement restrictions and more land grab. The

Jonam living on the Eastern bank of the River Nile were rounded up and forced across the river to the Western bank to farm on newly grabbed land as labourers. This event made Chief Jonam to call for another meeting in less than a year.

The collision came about like this: while still at the meeting, a message was delivered to Chief Jonam of new land confiscation and arrests, including women, and children spearheaded by Coope. Upon receipt of the news chief Jonam stormed out of the meeting in protest and headed straight to the detention center to demand for the release of women and children. Unfortunately, none of the detainees was freed.

In the middle of the night Chief Jonam met with many youths and instructed them to take actions. At around 12:30am a ferry was set ablaze by group of disgruntled youths who were increasingly getting dissatisfied by the inability of their fathers to defend their freedoms and that of their mothers and siblings. Acres of cotton plantations nearing harvest were uprooted. News of the damages reached Mr. Edward who sent his emissaries to investigate the extent of the damages.

The relationship that had for many years been successful, somewhat collegial under the reign of Wadelai begun to deteriorate. The motives for the destruction of the cotton fields and burning of a ferry were presumably as confused in accessible and helpless in a chief as any of his subjects, but here are two which make sense: the inability of the colonial administration to deliver on the promises of a town, guns and economic liberation. Secondly, the indiscriminate land confiscation, hunting, logging of trees to almost extinction.

None of these reasons necessitated a revolt of Chief Jonam and the Youths, but there was a third that did, particularly the hanging of women, children and some of the Youth who were alleged to have spearheaded the burning of the ferry and uprooting of cotton plantations.

The situation was worsened by the blatant refusal to release the body of the hanged women and children to be given a decent burial. Instead the deceased were buried behind the Christian mission. In the days that followed, Mr. Edward invited Chief Jonam for dialogue at the Colonial administration headquarters. Intelligence information indicated that Chief Jonam was be detained and incarcerated to distant land if he had gone for a meeting at the suggested location.

Consequently Chief Jonam proposed a different meeting venue. He preferred the cotton plantation to which, Mr. Edward was much obliged. On the fateful afternoon, heavy dark clouds hang thick and low. Wind blew across the plantations. Uprooted dry cotton leaves raced across the field as if they were competing for one hundreds (100) meter's race.

While at the cotton plantation, the two men walk in the field to assess the extent of the damage and finally agreed to sit under a tree. Mr. Edward, who was not a good communicator, asked chief Jonam to denounce violence, rebellion and to instruct his subjects to respect colonial property, including cotton fields. But, Jonam reiterated his demand, calling for the immediate release of his subjects.

Jonam who had witnessed how his father's powers could be turned on and off by the colonial administration had developed a disinclination on the part of administration to having his powers turned on and off like a tap. In Chief Jonam's view, Mr. Edward had the latitude and was well placed to influence the behaviour of his officers, collaborator and turn around the situation.

Since, most of the sub-chiefs were beginning to resist the inhuman torture and ill treatment, Chief Jonam found that several complains had been waged for many years in favour of the removal of forced labour and the indiscriminate killing of the wild game. He saw that the future of his subjects was in danger. Chief Jonam! Are you with me, Mr. Edward inquired. Definitely, Chief Jonam's spirit had left him. A few minutes later, Mr. Jonam tries to flee the scene while Mr. Edward body lay on the ground with his head cut - off. As he raced towards the river in an attempt to catch a canoe to an unknown destination. He was intercepted and arrested by the colonial guards. That same day, Chief Jonam was transferred to Kampala to face trial.

In Kampala, Lord Guy was appointed to preside over the case with strict instructions. Upon arrival in Luzira prison, Chief Jonam was arranged before Lord Guy. In normal court proceedings every criminal defendant is supposed to be presumed innocent until proven guilty. The standard of proof is supposed to be beyond a reasonable doubt. A preponderance of evidence, as used in civil proceedings is not sufficient to sustain a criminal conviction. Also, the burden of proof is on the public prosecutor. He had to establish every element of the offence beyond a reasonable doubt, otherwise Chief Jonam must be acquitted or convicted only for a lesser included offence.

Lord Guy exploited the maxim, a defendant has rights to a speedy and public trial by an impartial tribunal as provided for in colonial law. The trial was supposed to be conducted and judgement announced publicly. But, Lord Guy opted for the exception which permitted announcements in closed set under very limited circumstances.

The trials opened with the judges and a public

prosecutor in attendance. Lord Guy asked the public prosecutor to make an opening statement. To explain the evidence and what is intended to be proven. When it was time for the defendants lawyer to speak, there was no defense lawyer to explain flaws in prosecution case, lay out contradicting evidence, alternate theory of the crime. Chief Jonam remained silent during most part of the trial but only responded occasionally. Chief Jonam was deprived of the right to be assisted by a competent counsel. Since he was unable to secure a competent counsel, the court should have appointed a counsel to represent him.

Chief Jonam's trial proceeded without the presence of a counsel. He was charged with an offence punishable by death. There was no direct examination by prosecutor to question witness, tell story of events, lay out the crime and evidence to support prosecution's theory of case. Also, no cross examination by defense to question each prosecution witness, discredit witness character assassination. The prosecution delivered its closing statement but there was no closing statement by defense. The Judge reviewed all laws with jury and what they can convict defendant of, possible punishment. In his final verdict, Lord Guy sentenced Chief Jonam to death.

From the Court room, Chief Jonam was led straight to the execution machine room. Therein, he was tied and slid into the machine while his son Kush, brother valente and other relatives witnessed. He kept singing as the machine consumed him starting with his legs. Kush joined his father and sung with him. Kush attempted to jump into the machine but was restrained by his uncle. Chief Jonam's body had been turned into crushed flesh, a scene so horrifying that Kush and Valente sobbed that whole afternoon. The next day, Kush and Valente traveled back to Wadelai.

The news of Chief Jonam's death paralyzed activities in Wadelai. A mammoth crowd of mourners gathered to give their fallen chief a befitting burial. The situation was so tense that the colonial administration officials had to call for reinforcement. After some years, the colonial government post was withdrawn.

Upon the high bank of the Nile River stood a long row of tall, peaked thatched houses, the wall of a fort, building of British construction, which were laboriously build maintained. The half a Century of effort, experiment and spectacle of civilization and the once admired Wadelai spacious landscape, with its green expanses, its lofty peaks, its trees, its venture rising from the mighty and majestic river was free at last. The freedom of Wadelai came at a heavy price.

Since then, the Jonam people continued to live, fish

and farm on both sides of the River Nile in present day Pakwach and Amuru districts. These districts continue to be affected by politics of land tenure. The question of land tenure has become a critical and sensitive political issue in contemporary history of Jonam and Uganda.

In view of the agrarian and fishing nature of the society and the crucial function of rural land as an essential economic resource in this community, it is no – longer astonishing that land tenure has become a controversial political issue that involves not only opposing observations but also conflict of interests.

Crucially, agriculture and fishing continues to be the back born of Jonam's economy. It is the major source of livelihood and income security for approximately 90 percent of the people. Agriculture is a vital source of raw materials for small, medium and large scale industries as well as being the main source of foreign exchange earnings.

This play is an attempt to advocate for Jonam people's rights to land in the land tenure systems from 1962 to the land legal reform of 1998 and the current tenure policy.

This account of the Chief Wadelai as I wrote: what compelled me was an individual who could not be accused of xenophobia, who indeed seized life in great variety and who welcomed and cherished prosperity. Who nevertheless found something in himself without which life was meaningless. His unwavering openness and hospitality rendered to European visitors turned masters later haunted him. When the colonial administrators backtracked on their promise on a town, guns and prosperity.

For Chief Jonam, upholding his father's aspiration to maintain resistance in defense of his mother land to sustain the existence of his future generation. He was willing to dialogue with his colonizers for the betterment of his society. Of course his disagreements were associated; the indiscriminate hunting, land confiscation, logging and forced labour to which he was opposed.

But, I think Chief Jonam would have found his way around on how to address these issues amicably. He showed every sign of doing so through his acceptance to attend all consultation meetings. Unfortunately, his call for the release of his detained subjects, immediate return of confiscated land and forced labour were blatantly rejected.

Another character that attracted me was Kush, an amazing and splendid man, and ability to social adjustment. A graduate and respectful son of a chief. He was an admired man, adored by the Jonam people. I see, I have used a lot of African anecdotes in the play. I know no other way to treat this subject. In the play I also use imagery. The references to ferry, rivers, cotton, logging and so on are all used for this purpose.

I set out with no very well formed idea of the kind of play it was to be, except that it was not to be natural. The possibility of using imagery that is of using African anecdotes not decoratively but with an interior way is a side effect of that. It is perhaps necessary to add that by a play i mean something clear-cut not something reflective.

THE TRAILS OF JONAM was first presented by Matthew Wedgwood and Santamaria Blacwood at BT Cineplex, Kampala, Uganda, on May 30, 2020, with the following cast:

(IN ORDER OF APPEARANCE)

Lapeny:	Meg Lapeny
Wadelai:	Chief Wadelai
Makmot:	Andre Makmot
Watmon:	Dez Watmon
Pasquale:	Pasquale Moi
Tawona:	Tamara Tawona
Tekakwo:	Acellam Tekakwo
Latim:	Moses Latim
Sergeant:	John Rwakasanga
Lord Guy:	Tim Sessions
Jason:	Hart Chris
Chief Jonam:	Luke Jonam
Kush:	Coming Odokomit
Wader:	Bless Amooti
Nakimera:	Tamara Nakimera
Steward:	Clement Ofwono
Valente:	Valente Oliya
Fasika:	Fasika Akullu
Driver:	Moses Data
Passenger:	Musoke Blanc
Coope:	Galileo Coope
Priest:	Dino Okumu
Odwel:	John Odwel
Jacan:	Jacan James

Longoro:	Troy Longoro
Alonyo:	Valerie Alonyo
Krishna:	Krishna Aman
Celina:	Celina Akullo
Anyango:	Anyango Meg
Atuku:	Atuku Sharon
Otim:	Otim Nimrod
Ber-iwu:	Ber-Iwu Theodros
Nimungu:	Alfa Nimungu

PEOPLE IN THE PLAY

Lapeny: Early thirties. She wears a kitenge from head to bottom which delineate her splendid figure. Her face is colored in the black, yellow and Red. It's a symbol of national unity and independence.

Wadelai: Late Seventies. Eloquent, respectful and humble. The Lion of the land and Son of the burning spear. He often talks about Jonam Unity and the evils of disunity.

Makmot: Old. Very liberal and a good listener. He is Chief Wadelai's handler and trusted lieutenants. Loves to wear his blue pair of sandals and dotted court. Respected for his wit and cultural values. He is the spokesperson of the chiefdom and head of the sub-chiefs.

Watmon: Late seventies. Very ruthless, loudmouth with excellent intellect. A strong believer in tradition and takes issues head on. He is known for inheriting widows. He is obedient and observes all commands. He is known for his time management and strict adherence to command.

Pasquale: Eighties. Remorseless, hard -hearted, merciless, unrelenting and easily angered. Though, he always wears a smile on his face even in very tough situation. Dressed in a brown court and black trousers. He once slapped a white man for allegedly insulting his mother. He was detained but later released.

Tawona: Mid-Thirties. Dressed in a kitenge. She is very loquacious and funny. A lady of high moral fortitude and resilience. She is bitter about the fate of her mother and siblings. She dances at functions and ceremonies for living. She misses her father who was killed by an elephant during a hunting exercise.

Tekakwo: Early sixties. Very discreet, tactful, enigmatic, risk adverse and proud of his brainpower. He is an advisor to Chief Wadelai on all matters of the chiefdom and engagements with sister chiefdoms and kingdoms. He is determined to get rich at all cost. He is very assiduous and explores business opportunity.

Latim: Late fifties. Skinny, energetic and enthusiastic. Dressed in black shirt and white trousers and a pair of torn shoes. A strong advocate of an independent Wadelai free from colonial administrators exploitation. Appears troubled by his inability to change the situation.

Sergeant: Late twenties: A soldier body held together by rigid adherence to the minimal code of conventional duty. Aware of his moral and command assignment.

Lord Guy: Late fifties. He is subtle and very serious. His facial expression does not exhibit any inner tension but incredible out-going will of duty. A self-conceit that can cradle gross crimes in the name of effective action. In sum an intellectual bully and a stout follower of the law in letter and spirit.

Jason: Middle thirties. He is heavy and unexercised. A studious unhappy face and wears hatred for any behaviour deemed dangerous towards the government. He is an academic hounded by self-doubt to be in the community and seeks to uplift himself from self - doubt.

Chief Jonam: Late fifties. Wears a decayed body and hairy face. Espouses a better future for his Jonam people. Very ambitious with excellent intellect, he now wears a lonely regret of self-indulgence and contempt. He is prayerful after dropping his ancestral spirits in favor of Christian faith.

Kush: Late twenties. He appears lazy but the life of the mind in him is so abundant. He is often staggering but never wild and posses natural moderation attributes. He is armed with an excellent command of English. The face is intellectual and quickly delighted, easily aroused during crises but very compassionate.

Warder: Weighty, inactive, a guard held together by strict observance of command decision. Attractively aware of his surrounding and his moral. Intellectually insignificant but a good man. Always quiet but convinced that his ideas are imperative because they are his and applicable.

Nakimera: Late Twenties. A beautiful girl of high moral character. She wears an excellent command of English but also rich in tradition of her people and hospitable to strangers. She is very talkative and full of humor.

Steward: Sixties. Heavy and overweighed. Sharp-minded, sharp – faced. He is strong administrator and pays strict adherence to time. Appears sleepy most of the time, though, well vast with the historical features along the route. He is a mastery of local languages and Swahili.

Valente: Late forties. A professional teacher of good virtues. He is dressed in grey shirt and woolen trouser. Much on his dignity as a man of his word. He in fact trots happily but lost between tradition and contemporary discourse. Appears troubled by his inability to change his world and remove the unfreedom his people are living with daily.

Fasika: Old. A big decayed body. Always in Gomsi, a traditional wear. Her memory of tradition is unmatched but now wears a lonely life, especially after the untimely death of her husband. She is easily angered and always conveying instruction to her grandchildren and demands strict adherence to traditional values.

Driver: Early thirties. Always chewing. He possess a stiff body and immobile face. Poor command of English and a staunch admirer of Congolese music. Moderate brain, full of anecdote and traditional beliefs.

Passenger: Seventies. Looks remorseful, caring and a man of good family. Dressed in white shirt and brown Italian trouser and a pair of African sandals.

Coope: Early forties. Restless, cunning, sly but calm. His well-built in stature with a pot-belly and dressed in khaki pants, checked shirt and a cap. An ex-seminarian and boast of theological intellect but was unable to complete his theological studies. Expelled from the Seminary for slapping a deacon. He feels life has cheated him and wants to catch up with his mates. His love for wealth and power is so immense to the extent of betraying his kinsmen.

Priest: Late thirties. Humble, tact and sharp-faced. Sees himself as an intercessor and intermediary. Dressed in a white large flowing cassock, rosary and garments. He considers religious doctrines as a set of devices and church affairs as a profession of administration. He does not distinguish between personal issues and religious matters.

Odwel: Early fifties. Hard -hearted, unrelenting and easily angered. His comrades admire his hardworking attitude and trustworthiness. But, also his determination to succeed by all means. Loves wearing his shred trouser and bark cloth shirt. Owns acres of land and rents land to his displaced village mates.

Jacan: Late twenties. Very secretive, proud of his intellect, a crude businessman and thrifty. Always quiet but of good heart. Defensive, argumentative and believes he is always right. He strives to win all arguments at all costs. He is very industrious and indulges in any business opportunity.

Longoro: Early twenties. Skinny, active and a good listener. Dressed in a short and t-shirt. He rebelled against his father's position in the spirit of comradeship. A youth leader in his village. Famous for mobilizing the youth to rise up against forced labour.

Alonyo: Middle sixties. Self – opinionated. Dressed in kitenge and wears a head scuff. She has a good grasp of historical events and folklore. As a daughter of a former chief, she is a strict observer of traditional norms.

Krishna: Fifties. He calls himself an investor and entrepreneur. A risk taker and a master of more than eight native languages. His father was an Indian coolie. Very sinister and has been accused of acting as an agent of colonial administrators.

Celina: Middle forties. Dressed in black dress. Self-confident, and self-righteous, self-centered and proud. Boast of kingship ancestry and royalty. Detests weak and feeble characters.

Anyango: Late thirties. Born into an agricultural family. Now an educated lady. She is absurd at a distance, impressive close to. Loves fashion, she praises success, brave and hot-hearted. She loves her children and parents. In consequence, troubled by and defiant towards both. She is a strict disciplinarian and demands respect.

Atuku: Middle twenties. Very talkative and humorous. A beautiful lady of enthusiastic fineness; both suffers and shelters behind a reserved stillness. She worships her husband and mother.

Otim: Early forties. Brave, adventurous, argumentative and opinionated. A soldier body held together by rigid adherence to the minimal code of conventional duty. Sees himself as a liberator. Detest racial discrimination. He is relentless and pursues his dream and ready to confront obstacles head on. Though, he loves style, fashion and music. Seeks to uplift himself regardless of challenges that confront him.

Ber-iwu: Middle thirties. Heavy and overweighed. Sharp-minded, sharp – faced. Always, quiet, very secretive, risk adverse and proud of his intellect. He is a strong financial, administrator and loves accountability. Strict disciplinarian and respect individual boundaries.

Nimungu: Early thirties. Humorous, comical, witty and hilarious. Very ambitious with excellent numerical intellect and is always seen wearing his cow-boy hut. Loves his home land. Self-confident, self-righteous and undiminishing commitment to duty. He is also adventurous and a risk taker.

THE SET is the same throughout but capable of varies lightings, as indicated. It's a form is finally a matter of the designer, but to some extent is dictated by the action of the play. I have visualized on large curtains split into two, able to be entered from off-stage. A flight of stairs leading from both sides of the stage. A projection which can suggest a closet, with a another curtains on the sides and tapestry curtain to be drawn across it. A table and some chairs, sufficiently heavy to be congruous indoors or out.

THE CONSUMES are also a matter for the designer, but I have visualized no exact reproductions of the elaborate style of the period. I think a mix of grey, blue, white and red colors should be used, thus the different actors in the play will where these colour, except the use of black and white colours during court trials.

ACT ONE

When the door opens, the set is in a village homestead. But for one spot upon which Lapeny is standing while holding a local trumpet. He starts speaking...!

Wadelai is chief; Jonam is prince; Mego is Simba. It must be remembered that Wadelai is the Lion of the land. He often talks about Jonam Unity, talks about the evils of disunity. Mentioning that he did not know or had not known that his chiefdom was affiliated to Kabalega's kingdom. Son of the burning spear, must go on the hill top to tell his people to face the hills. I can see a series of bad happenings and invasions. I am here to open your eyes and warn you of the pain that is coming. I can see the son of the burning spear on top of the hill. People are going to face the hills but before we face the hills, let's face the river. It's the only means into Jonam land. What has happened to Coope. So close to power. Actually until only recently, the leading light on togetherness from our land. A person who seems set to represent Ojigo in our council of elders was impeached. Why was he impeached? Could it be that he was unpopular? Just yesterday, I spoke to senior elders from Ojigo and they told me, yes, Coope is so unpopular. He is just unpopular. Could it be that is the case? I don't know. Could it also be that someone is eyeing his seat? May be, may be not. Could it be that the wealthy Aligo, the great fisherman or the great hunter wants his seat and therefore stings trouble for him? May be, may be not. But that is not what my focus is. Some of those could be the reason but I doubt. What I want to bring out in a more general sense is that we are going to see pain and suffering happening.

I see our chief and his son hunting. They have surrounded the animal and battling with it alone. But am not seeing exactly the position of the animal. Either, the animal is still standing or its about to fall. The moment they fell the animal, if they haven't, done so. It is time for people to rush with their knives and therefore, I want to advise my elders to open some of their eyes, at least one, if they have two. God has been good to us and blessed us with animals, fertile land, the great River Nile, flora and fauna. If we don't make use of these opportunities to strengthen our defenses, someone else will come and exploit us. This is a season of practice and preparation. The moment the animal is cleared and the hunt is over. We must now reduce the number of dissenting views in the chiefdom to avoid outsiders from using them against us. Not everybody will be allowed to come near the animal with blunt knives.

Could it therefore be that since Coope hard worked himself into leadership position, he must be weeded out so that there is no threat for Prince Jonam to ascend the throne. Is it an elimination of a potential threat? If we investigate these by extension and move community by community, we could see this playing out. But my chief, do not remain silent. To agree to have dialogue is the beginning of a peaceful solution. We need alliances and cooperation with neighbouring chiefdoms and kingdoms. Isolation is the enemy of progress. When I see my people running like headless chicken and yet the enemy is at our door steps... I see our chiefs power removed, literally undressed and cold. I see our chief being given a dirty shirt. He is happy to wear it because he is cold. He can no-longer defend his people. He cannot claim a place at the table of men. So take the initiative to establish cooperation with other chiefdoms and kingdoms for the betterment of Jonam.

Get on the table, you will not survive or defend your people on your own. It might be viewed as a move out of desperation but the invaders and rent seekers are in alliance to fleece us all. I call upon you to go where men are and claim your place at the table and remember when the season of harvest is over. When the men at the table have harvested all they need and the Jonam people have been sidelined. You will watch from afar as the cooking continues in the kitchen. You will only see the smoke. In our language, we call it 'Yiro'. You will only see smoke coming out of the house but what is going on inside, you will not know. 'Rubanga' our God has blessed us with fertile soil, flora and fauna and the mighty river Nile but I see the rent seekers nearing.

During the last part of the speech, footsteps are heard approaching Chief Wadelai's house. There is a knock at the door.

Wadelai: Come in! Come in! (*door opens*). It's you my son. What brings you this early to my house? Is there a problem?

Jonam: Yes! Father. Good Morning?

Wadelai: (*Puzzled*). How was your night? Serve yourself some tea.

Jonam: (*Looking at the pot. Picks it and pours tea in a little clay cup and sips*). Father! Did you listen to the village emissary last night?

Wadelai: (*Surprised*). Oh Yes! So you were also awake late last night.

Jonam: Yes! Father. But, I am here for a different reason. I had a very terrible dream last night.

Wadelai: (*Baffled and perplexed*). Terrible dream! What was the dream about my son?

Jonam: In the dream, some foreigners came to our land. They were led by one of our kinsmen. You were arrested and put in prison. Therein, you fell sick and passed on.

Wadelai: (*Dumbstruck and shocked*). I rebuke the bad omen in the name of our forefathers. Anyway don't worry my son. It's just a dream.

Jonam: Father, why don't you summon Iapeny to elucidate and interpret her vision and message.

Wadelai: May be, she was drunk last night. Her head cannot accommodate Satan's tears.

Jonam: But, she sounded dead serious, father. I suggest you invite her for a meeting so that she can substantiate her message.

(A knock is heard at the door)

Wadelai: Jonam, go and check who is at the door.

Jonam: (*Opens the door*). Father! Its Coope. Please come in.

Coope: (*Very moody and glum*). No! I am here with new administrators. They urgently want to meet the Chief. Tell him that the visitors are waiting under the tree. He should come out at once.

Jonam: Father! Coope is here with strangers. He says they are new administrators and are waiting for you.

Wadelai: (*Surprised and stunned*). Tell them, I will be there in ten minutes.

Jonam: (*Walks out of the house*). Coope! Father says he will be with the visitors in ten minutes. Please inform them accordingly.

Coope: (*An amused and irritated*). I will deliver Chief's reply

Jonam: Okay, please entertain them

Coope: (*Contrite and kneeling*). Mister Edward, Chief Wadelai will be with us in a few minutes.

Edward: (Furious and raged). Few minutes! Who does he think he is? Let me go fetch him.

Edward walks towards Chief, Wadelai's house. Kicks the wooden door and the door flanks open. He is heard shouting at Chief. You are wasting everybody's time. Get out at once or face the consequences.

Wadelai: (*Terrified and in shock. Calmly walks out of his house towards the tree*). Coope, who are these people and what do they want from my land?

Coope: They found me fishing and asked me to bring them to our chief. Mr. Edward, I beg to take my leave. He is the Chief of this land.

Edward: You may leave. But, I want to see you first thing tomorrow morning.

Coope: Yes, I will be available.

Edward: Chief Wadelai, my name is Edward, the head of this contingent. With me are four teams, including hunters, loggers, miners and farmers and administrators. We are here with a specific mandate.

Wadelai: (*Wondering*). What is your mandate?

Edward: (*Passes a file full of document to chief Wadelai*). The document contains details of our mandate and expectations. Your people have a choice to cooperate or we use necessary force to make your people comply.

Wadelai: (*Speechless. He takes a heavy breath*). We can only cooperate for mutual benefits.

Edward: (*Wears a plastic smile*). Of course we will provide you with guns, monetary equivalent, jewelry for your women and transform Wadelai into a modern town in return.

Wadelai: (*Moved and visibly excited*). Well said, I will hold a meeting with all the sub-chiefs to convey the message to them and confirm their cooperation and commitment. We the Jonam people aspire for a modern town.

Edward: We will retire to the fort build by Governor Emin Pasha and rehabilitate it. I look forward to hearing from you soon.

Wadelai: Welcome to our land.

That same evening, the village emissary delivered invitations for a meeting the next day.

The meeting started at 10:00am the next day. During the meeting chief Wadelai briefed the council of elders on his deliberations with Mr. Edward.

Wadelai: Comrades! I greet you all in the name of our forefathers.

Gathering: Greetings to you our chief

Wadelai: A chief's wealth is his subjects.

Tekakwo: My people, why is chief Wadelai starting with a riddle today?

Wadelai: (*Jovial and Jocund*). I am speaking in proverbs so that he who is wise and intelligent will understand. Yesterday, Coope, led a group of strangers to our palace. Whereupon, I met with them. They informed me about their mandate and served me with a volume of documents. I wish my grandson was here. My eyes can see the white man's letters but cannot decipher their meanings. Their leader informed me that his team is made up of four

36

groups, including hunters, loggers, miners and farmers. Also, they stated that they will undertake this undertakings with or without our cooperation. However, they said if we cooperate, Wadelai will be transformed into a modern town, our women will wear modern beads and jewelry. We will receive guns to defend ourselves and many other things. We will also receive monetary rewards for our labour. Therefore, you have to mobilize the people to produce cotton, groundnuts, hunt elephants and Rhinos for their tusks, log trees for timber and mine minerals. I thank you for listening. Your comments and observations are welcome.

Pasquale: (*Not amused. His voice is coarse and abrasive*). Comrades! A wrong step by a leader is a warning to his followers. Chief, do you trust these people? I saw them yesterday from a hideout. They look suspicious, potential looters and imperialist. Remember, the story we were told about their activities in Bunyoro and Buganda kingdoms after they were welcomed. To me Lapeny's warning will soon come to pass. I think the devil is in the details of the documents given to chief.

Gathering: (*Applause in agreement with Pasquale's submissions*). Yes, we should heed to Lapeny's warnings.

Wadelai: (*Wittingly*). Pasquale! Our people say, 'a mouse that makes a jest of a cat has already seen a hole nearby. Do we have an alternative?

Tekakwo: Chief Wadelai, you have spoken well. An egg cannot stage in a fight with a rock. We must prepare and build our capability so that we can withstand wrath of the devil. Without spiritual powers we cannot confront the devil or attempt to chase an evil spirit. Otherwise, we will be crashed.

Wadelai: If we do not seize this opportunity today, we may be unable to seize tomorrows opportunity. I promised to meet Mr. Edward today to report the outcome of our deliberations and how we will support his team to meet their targets.

Pasquale: Chief Wadelai, I don't want to sound rude. But, we need to have a written agreement with these looters. I don't trust these men. The way they kicked your door means they are capable of even killing you. They disrespected you as our chief.

Tekakwo: (*Known for his inconsistencies*). I agree with you Pasquale. Chief should ask for an agreement spelling out the terms of our cooperation.

Gathering: Absolutely! A Memorandum of Understanding is a requirement.

Wadelai: Comrades! I will explore possibilities of signing a memorandum of understanding for a specified period and revert to you.

Gathering: Wonderful! Long live our chief.

Wadelai: I propose that we divide ourselves in four groups. So starting with Pasquale, lets count one, two, three and four. Then, starting again with Tekakwo, one, two, three..... and all the sub-chiefs were divided into four groups.

All members of group one will work with the hunting team. Group two will work with logging team. While group three will grow cotton and group four grow groundnuts. A small team will work with the miners. I think all is set?

Gathering: Yes!

Wadelai: I would like to appreciate you all for your cooperation. Have a good evening.

Gathering: Long live our chief.

The next morning chief wadelai, paid a visit to the colonial fort at Wadelai to meet with Mr. Edward.

Edward: Good Morning, Chief.

Wadelai: Good Morning, Edward

Edward: How did your meeting go yesterday?

Wadelai: (*With a smile on his face*). Oh, it proceeded very smoothly. We were able to form four groups, including hunting, logging, farming and mining groups. The sub-chiefs have welcomed the idea of transforming Wadelai into a town. However, they requested a Memorandum of Understanding to spell out the terms and conditions of our engagement.

Edward:	(*Uncomfortable and disturbed*). A memorandum of Understanding. For what? Why do we need one? Chief, the earlier your people understand the better. This request should never be repeated.
Wadelai:	(*In attempt to change the course of the conversation*). So when will the ferry arrive.
Edward:	November this year. We expect by that time all the required quantities are gathered.
Wadelai:	(*Uneasy but stable*). Absolutely! I will ensure each sub-chief delivers on his target as per the specifications. The items will be readily available by November.
Edward:	Have a good day chief.

In the first season, the Jonam people pursued money. As one elder put it, '*money is sharper than a sword*'. Thousands of elephant and Rhino tusks, logs, tons of cotton and bags of ground nuts were collated and stored in readiness to be ferried.

November came and the ferry arrived with a cargo which was promptly offloaded. The next day, several youths were mobilized to reload the ferry enroute to Europe via Sudan and Egypt.

A week, later Chief Wadelai decided to visit Edward to follow up on the promises and payments for labourers who loaded the goods on the ferry.

Wadelai: (*Still looking sleepy*). Morning! My people are still waiting and expecting monetary equivalent for their labour.

Edward: (*Perturbed and nervous*). Inform your people. Patience is the key which solves all problems. When the ferry returns next November. The promises will be delivered. The goods enroute to Europe will be sold and the returns will be employed to reward your people. Please inform them.

Wadelai: (*Dissatisfied with the response*). I will inform my people accordingly.

In evening, Chief Wadelai's village emissary delivered invitation to sub-chiefs for a meeting the next day. The meeting commenced at 11:30am.

Wadelai: Comrades! Greetings

Gathering: (*Feeble in their reply*). Greetings our chief.

Wadelai: (*Staring into the sky*). No matter how long the night is, the day is sure to come. Yesterday, I met with Mister Edward, he informed me that the goods we have sent to Europe have to be sold then the returns will be delivered when the ferry returns in November. Each of you will be adequately compensate for your hard work and labour. Your comments and observations are welcome.

Tekakwo: My people. He who asks questions is never wrong. For the sake of peace, hard decisions must be made! How shall we hold these people accountable without a signed agreement or Memorandum of Understanding?

Gathering: Accountability! Are we not being duped?

Latim: (*Angry and vile*). Let us attack and burn

their fort down. My brother and nephew who were part of the hunting group were killed by elephants. My relatives cannot die in vain.

Wadelai: Comrades! You all know that annoyance burned the chief's house. Since work is the medicine of poverty. Let's not be like the cow that delivered a premature calf. We are about to succeed. let us not lose hope and focus.

Pasquale: (*Not convinced*). It's all a magicians show. These people are like pepper, not until you chew it, you will not know how hot it is. Let us be real, they bring their food from out of our community. How can they promote our transformation with these mentality. If we want peace, we should prepare to defend ourselves. Let's open our eyes.

Wadelai: (*Concedes*). It's true that a fish and bird may fall in love but the two cannot build a home together. I beseech you all to wait until November. This new season, lets produce two folds. On a different note, my grandson Kush has successfully completed his bachelor degree and he will return soon so we can celebrate.

Lapeny:	Kush was away in Kampala for a little under three years. He sometimes found it difficult to believe that it was as short as that. It seems more like a decade than three years. With his studies associated loneliness then his longing to see his grandpa and father Jonam and mother.
	Going from Kampala to Wadelai was like going from trade show to funeral. For all its modern flats and its expensive landscape, wadelai was like a graveyard.
	He took a favorite seat in the bus, just behind the driver's seat then he saw a young lady in her early twenties boarding the same bus. Coincidently, she sat next to him.
Kush:	Good morning maiden, smiling broadly.
Draru:	Good morning. How are you?
Kush:	Fair, I got mild headache.
Draru:	Oh, I have some painkillers, they might help.

Kush:	Thank you for the tablets (*He placed two tablets and starting to chew*)
Draru:	(*After 30 minutes*) did they make you feel better.
Kush:	Yes, very much. (*Kush, leaned on the window to watch the distant hills that seemed to race in the opposite direction*).
Passenger:	Walking to the back, slid and fell
Kush:	I'm sorry.
Passenger:	Oh, it's nothing (*laughing foolishly and went his way to the back*).
Kush:	I nearly fell myself
Draru:	You need to be careful
Driver:	(*Announcement*). We are approaching Luwero. We will have a 10 minutes stopover.
Kush:	Do you like to have some 'Gonja' (*roasted plantain*).
Draru:	Sure! Just two pieces.
Kush:	What drink will you have? There is

coca cola, Pepsi, and Mirinda.

Draru: Pepsi, please, it's getting rather warm. (*She drew her thumb across her face and flicked the sweat away*).

Kush: It is indeed getting hot, isn't it. (*Blowing into his chest*). What is your surname, by the way. Mine is Kush.

Draru: Mine is Draru.

Kush: Draru is a fine name. What does it mean. I am told all our names have meanings.

Draru: Well, I don't know.

Kush: What are you studying at the University?

Draru: Social work, why?

Driver: (*Announcement*). We are approaching Pakwach. We will have 15 minutes stopover.

Kush: Oh, I just wanted to know. How old are you? Excuse me for my being so inquisitive.

Draru: Twenty three and you?

Kush: Twenty six. But, you look sweet
            sixteen.

Draru: (*Smiling*). Oh really. what did you
            study at the University?

Kush: English literature. I fact, I was sent to
            study law but I changed my mind and
            decided to study English literature.

Draru: (*Surprised*). Why? Law is highly rated
            course.

Kush: So that I can assist my community to
            relate with the colonial administrators
            who are stationed at the fort in
            Wadelai.

Draru: Colonial Administrators. What are
            they doing there?

Kush: Oh! They have set up a fort in Wadelai.
            They are involved in many activities,
            including hunting, mining, logging
            and farming. They are fleecing my
            people.

Draru: So sad! We are a bit lucky, they have
            no base in our village.

Kush:	We shall overcome. They have been logging and killing elephants and Rhinos for decades. I don't know what our future generations will experience.
Draru:	Its very sad. What are your leaders doing to change and rescue the plight of the your people.
Kush:	Several of my sub-chiefs who have challenged the status quo are behind bars. Others have disappeared.
Driver:	(*Announcement*). We are approaching Ojigo. All those disembarking ensure that you take all your belongings with you.
Kush:	Ms. Draru, it was nice meeting you. I will stop here and get other means to Mutir.
Draru:	Oh! I thought you were going to Arua. It was nice meeting you. May be, we will meet in the near future.
Kush:	Bye!
Draru:	Good bye!

Kush, disembarks from the bus. He found his father waiting for him.

Kush: (*Excited and enthusiastic*). Good afternoon, father!

Jonam: Welcome! My son. How was your journey?

Kush: Fantastic! How is grandpa, mother and my siblings.

Jonam: They are all well and in good health.

Coope: Hey! Brothers.

Jonam: (*Aggressive and repugnant*). Who is your brother? So you think you can barge into my father's chieftaincy and steal the throne from me. Ah!

Kush: Like a thief in the night.

Coope: It's like you both are into drugs. There is something you smoke which has got into your heads. What rubbish are you talking about the throne? and who even told you I am interested in the throne?

Jonam: (*Still obnoxious and distasteful*). Look at

this pretender. Look at this worse pretender. Look, Coope, or whatever they call you. As long as we the members of this chieftaincy are concerned. You are nothing but a gold digger. My friend get out from here. Get out of my sight. Oh! so you think you can come and reap from where you did not sow. Nonsense, good for nothing. Coope! Stay out of my way.

Coope: (*Unamused and shocked*). You stay out of my way, you both. Okay! The fact that I am quiet does not mean, I am a weakling. If you do not stay out of my path, I will smash you both.

Kush: I will slice you like papaya. You touch my father. Coope! You think you have power? You think you have influence? We will show you, why we are called grandsons of the burning spear. Can you imagine this village lumpen.

Coope: The reason I am having this conversation with you in the first place, is simply because of my father's relationship with Wadelai. Else, I will crash you and make you both disappear.

Jonam: (*Mocking*). Eh! Ha-ha-ha... Kush! Did
              you hear him, ha-ha-ha..., I will make
              you disappear, look!...look at this
              thing.

Coope: (*Warning*). You both don't know who I
              am.

Jonam: You are a product of one night stand.
              You gold digging tool, come and take
              the throne. Coope, do you know who
              you are talking too? "...I am the angel
              of death" ha-ha-ha, look at this one
              night stand. Ha-ha-ha...

Coope: I will show you, what a product of one
              night stand can do. Soon you will
              know why I am called 'dongini riyo', a
              snake with two heads.

Jonam: What is the meaning of this nonsense
              you just said.

Coope: Oh, I see you did not comprehend.
              Look at this no brainers.

Jonam: I can see you have grown wings. I
              mean you are not yet chief and you
              have started to threaten the son and
              grandson of the burning spear, eh!

53

Coope:	Is it not you who begun. I greeted you and you started the exchange. Are you going to fight the son of this land?
Kush:	Who is the son of the air? ha-ha-ha... Coope! You make me laugh. You product of one night stand. Son of a grave digger. Oh, you think you can be chief over us? You! Very soon, I will send you to 'Limbo' where you belong, if my father fails.
Coope:	The Chieftaincy of Wadelai is where I belong and nobody, not even both of you can do anything about it.
Jonam:	Look! Coope or whatever, they call you. Let me warn you. Do not go ahead with your sinister motives. A few decades ago, you brought foreigners to my father's house. You continue to cooperate with these colonialist against your people. You are responsible for the suffering of our people. All the trees we used in the past for making canoes are gone, White Rhino's have been depleted as reported by the hunters. The elephants are soon facing the same fate. Do you see what your betrayal has caused?

Coope:	(*Itimango*). What will you do?
Jonam:	Because, if you continue, I will commit a crime in this land. I can promise you. I will deal with your master soon.
Coope:	There comes a time in a man's life when he has to fight for what he believes in. that time is now.
Jonam:	Hmmm! You see this boy. You will never win. This fight will consume you. Look, let me tell you. What do you want, as far as am concern, your threat won't push me an inch.
Coope:	(*Furious*). I dare you. I dare you both to do your worst. Jonam! Jonam! How many times have I called your name? If you don't know who you are talking too. I am the son of this soil. Do you know a place called Luzira? That is where you will end up. I dare you to foment trouble. You cannot not threaten me.
Jonam:	(*Agitated and seethed*). Kush, let's go home. We will see who is who.
	A reception is set up to welcome and celebrate Kush who has completed his

studies from the University.

Wadelai: (*Jovial and blithe as sub-chiefs are eating*). As I have bought it all and you people are eating that is my job.

Gathering: Long live our chief. We are feeding because you are the provider.

Wadelai: Yes! Yes! Go on and eat and there will be more from where this one came from.

Makmot: Chief! Chief! We appreciate your generosity. I wonder what we would be without you.

Wadelai: You see. Nothing gives me more joy than being with you all. At last I have been able to sell that widows land at an exorbitant amount to a potential businessman. It was a huge sum of money.

Gathering: Eh...!

Wadelai: Do you understand and you know what gives me joy also. Is to see my sub-chiefs happy. Henceforth, all our meetings will be like this.

Gathering: Our chief, may you live long.

Wadelai: As we are talking, we are eating. As we are eating, we are drinking, ha-ha-ha. Let's enjoy ourselves.

Tekakwo: Chief! Why did God bless us with a chief like you? What did we do? A chief like you who is taking good care of us like this. May you live long.

Pasquale: Chief, permit me to ask this elders just one question.

Wadelai: Go ahead, the oracle of Oliya.

Pasquale: Have you seen any community within us or around us sitting with their chief and enjoying the way we are enjoying every market day?

Watmon: (*Interjects*). Pasquale! Have you forgotten that the sub-chief of Ojigo chased away two of his council members just for failing to bring five liters of Kwete. Ha-ha-ha… How can you compare him to our chief?

Gathering: Ha-ha-ha, it's a joke.

Wadelai: My elders, there is money in this

house. Your chief has money. As long as this money is still coming. As long as I keep making this money. As long as the promises from the colonial administrators comes. You people will keep enjoying.

Gathering: He-he-he…hi-hi-hi. long live our chief.

Wadelai: Soon or even later today, my grandson, Kush will return from Kampala where he has been pursuing his degree studies at the University. His father Jonam has gone to receive him from Ojigo. Once he is here, I will start to teach him as I did to his father on our tradition, including how to take care of the elders of the chiefs council.

Gathering: Ha-ha-ha… he-he-he

Wadelai: ha-ha-ha… so eat, eat he-he-he

Makmot: May be our grandson has read all the books in the University. Ha-ha-ha…

Wadelai: wuuh! It's you people who have made the dry fish turn soft and delicious.

Gathering: (*Laughter*). Ha-ha-ha…hi-hi-hi…

Wadelai:	Eeh...! Makmot, Watmon, Tekakwo, Pasquale, today is a rainy day. It's not that you have eaten. It's not that you have drunk, there is money even after this pay, we shall continue to eat and drink. Here is a bundle for each of you.
Makmot:	Thank you chief. Let me keep mine first then distribute to the rest of my colleagues.
Watmon:	Makmot, pass mine. Chief! May you never lack.
Pasquale:	Chief! Yes, mine is in my hand. Of course it's going straight into my pocket.
Gathering:	(Laughter). Ha-ha-ha...Hi-hi-hi...
Wadelai:	Makmot, give Tekakwo the whole bag. Ha-ha-ha... Hi-hi-hi...
Makmot:	Let me keep the bag and give him the money.
Tekakwo:	Chief! May you reign be long.
Wadelai:	Makmot! Keep the bag, we will buy another one next time. What is remaining now is the celebration later

today when my grandson arrives. I hear the maidens have prepared very beautiful songs and dances to grace the occasion.

Makmot: Yes! The maiden are ready. In fact my daughter told me they want to make it colourful.

Wadelai: Makmot, please check who is at the door. There is a knock at the door.

Makmot: Oh, Chief, Jonam and Kush have arrived.

Wadelai: (*Exceedingly happy and tipsy*). Oh, my grandson, welcome back and congratulations upon your successful graduation. Today is a special day in our chiefdom. How was your journey?

Kush: Thank you Grandpa. My trip was good. I thank God for safe journey masses.

Gathering: Welcome our grandson and congratulation.

Wadelai: I can hear musical instruments outside. Let's go and join the ceremony. People have waited for long.

The ceremony was very colourful. In attendance were the sub-chiefs and Jonam people. One of the girls, a daughter to the widow whose land was sold by Chief Wadelai danced so well that Chief Wadelai was filled with joy.

Wadelai: (*Overwhelmed and joyous*). This is very good, beautiful, very beautiful.

Gathering: (*Applause*). Wonderful. Well done our daughter.

Wadelai: Oh yes, beautiful dance. The girl has danced well. She has impressed my heart. My elders!

Gathering: (*Applause*). Yes our chief

Wadelai: My People.

Gathering: (*Applause*). Yes our Chief.

Wadelai: You have a chief that makes things happen. My daughter made me very happy. You have moved your chiefs heart to the extent that I wish to hereby declare that. Whatever it is that you wish, say it. Be it money, land or house. It shall be yours. Even half of my chiefdom.

Tawona: Our chief, you're a man of your own words.

Wadelai: Yes, I am a man of my own words.

Tawona: My Chief, I want the heart of Jonam together with his head.

Wadelai: (*Visibly in shock*). What did you say?

Tawona: (*Unwavering and resolute*). I want his heart and head.

Gathering: Wuweh! Aah… horror.

Tawona: Remove his heart and cut his head and give it to me.

Wadelai: (*In disbelief*). What?

Jonam: (*Furious and angry*). It is your heart and head that will be removed. Are you crazy or what?

Wadelai: (*Appealing to the girl to change her choice*). My daughter, what manner of desire? What manner of wish is that?

Tawona: Chief, in the next two market days, my
            mother and I will be waiting for you
            and Jonam in the forest where we live
            since you and the colonial
            administrator confiscated and sold my
            father's land. Bring his heart and head
            to me or your chiefdom will
            disintegrate and get destroyed by the
            enemies living next to your
            homestead.

Makmot: It's you who will be torn apart. Chief
            forget this young girls wish. Chief, the
            gathering will now disperse.

Wadelai: Sure! Everyone is free to leave. Many
            thanks for coming.

Jonam: Father, how could you make such a
            promise?

Wadelai: I did not know. She was the daughter
            of that wicked widow.

Jonam: You did not know because you are
            always open minded that is why the
            Colonial administrators exploited
            your openness to undermine and
            usurp your powers and confiscate our
            land, log at will and kill our fauna

almost to extinction.

Kush: Grandpa! What was the meaning of that? How could you make such a promise in this era. If my father is beheaded then who will be your successor? You know in our tradition, a chief cannot go back on his promise.

Jonam: I cannot die before accomplishing my mission of getting kicking Mr. Edward and his administrators out of our land. You better give your heart and head father.

Kush: My father cannot die for just a dance. I will hunt that girl and her mother if you don't take action grandpa.

Wadelai: Jonam, call for me all the chiefs for an urgent meeting tomorrow morning at 10:00am.

Jonam: Yes, father consider it done.

Wadelai: Its late, go to bed all of you.

Curtain

Wadelai:	(*He is troubled*). My sub-chiefs!
Gathering:	Yes, our chief.
Wadelai:	Yesterday was every unfortunate situation. I need a solution to this my problem.
Makmot:	Chief! You have to think first before saying anything. Why would you make such a promise you know you will not fulfill as the chief of this chiefdom.
Watmon:	Exactly! Chief, I cannot imagine anything, I can do. Whatever comes out of it. You must do it out of your own initiative. You will have to carry your own cross. As for me, I am living. (*He gets up and walks out of the meeting*)
Pasquale:	Oh Yes, Chief, you have to solve it yourself that is the only way out. I will not suffer for your mistake. I am living too.
Makmot:	Chief, I think we will have to go. You just have to think for away on how to solve this problem.

(*The remaining elders all walk out, leaving the chief alone*)

Wadelai: (*Still sitting. Starts to call*). Jonam, Jonam, Kush. Where are you?

Kush: Grandpa! Here I am.

Wadelai: Go and call your father. Tell him to come at once.

Kush: Oh, Grandpa, he is already here.

Jonam: Father, what is the issue. I heard you call my name.

Wadelai: All my chiefs have deserted me. I want a solution to yesterday's problem. What can we do?

Kush: Grandpa! That is why I did not want any ceremony but you people insisted. Now see what problem it has brought.

Jonam: So father, you have called me so that we can go to the forest to be beheaded.

Kush: No! Father, you cannot be beheaded. It's not possible. Grandpa! my father will not die. How could you make such a promise.

Wadelai: (*Talking to himself and asking questions*). Why me? Why did I do this? How did I come about making this promise. Rain beats a leopard's skin, but it does not wash out the spots. Son! We can do something. Go and gather some men. You are an old broom. Water always finds a way out.

Jonam: Yes, father I will act accordingly. The child of a lion is a lion.

Next day, Jonam returns home.

Jonam: Father, when bad luck chooses you as a companion, even a ripe banana can remove your teeth. But, we managed to turn the tide and completed the assignment.

Wadelai: (*Extremely ecstatic*). Well done my son. You are indeed a descendant of the burning spear.

Jonam: But, the men reported that they saw a ferry docking at the bank of river Nile yesterday. May be you need to follow

	up with Mr. Edward on the promises to our people.
Wadelai:	Oh really, I will arrange to meet him first thing tomorrow morning. Please prepare for me the necessary information for the meeting.
Jonam:	I will later. Father, Kush and I are going to fish and will return later today.
Wadelai:	Take care. The river sometimes gets rough.

The next morning Chief Wadelai, decided to pay Edward a visit to follow up on the promises made in the last calendar year.

Wadelai:	Greetings! Have my people's considerations been delivered.
Edward:	What is good about today? I am fed up of seeing your face. Please leave my sight. Before, I order the guards to arrest you.
Wadelai:	(*Not distracted*). I am here to follow up on commitments made to my people.

	They deserve to be compensated for their labour. It's now several decades and your answer has been the same.
Edward:	So, you did not hear me. Do you expect your master to pay you for working for him. The earlier you get this into your people's head the better. There will be no compensation for anybody. Get out of my sight or else, you will be locked up.
Wadelai:	Even, a donkey kicks its master, whenever, its overloaded. I will inform my people.
	At 2:00pm, all invited sub-chiefs are sitting under a tree shade in Chief Wadelai's compound.
Wadelai:	Comrades! Our people say, if you show off your strength, you will start a battle. Yesterday, I met with this people who call themselves our masters. I don't know who anointed them masters of men. They made statement that made me not to sleep. One of them said, how can I expect payment from my masters. There is no considerations for our several decades labour.

Makmot: Chief! There are guards surrounding us. Are we safe. I can see more guards coming from the fort. We are under cordon. Oh, Coope is among them.

Jonam: Coope! So you are at it again. Let me warn you. If you do not instruct these guards to leave my father's compound, I will do something very terrible in this land.

Coope: Guards, arrest all of them immediately and make sure they are all locked up in the detention room at the fort.

Wadelai: (*Perplexed and speechless*). Why are we being arrested? What crime did we commit?

Edward: We have received intelligence information that you are planning to sabotage development undertakings. Secondly, you will all be detained and will only be released if denounce resistance and your demand for compensation. If you denounce resistance then you will be set free.

            All the chiefs except Pasquale and Tekakwo and Wadelai, were set free after denouncing resistance and taking an oath never to demand for compensation.

Wadelai: (*Three hour before mid-night*) Tekakwo, I feel one side of my body is frozen and painful. I can't breathe. Please ask for help.

Makmot: Guards! Chief Wadelai needs medical attention. Please inform Mr. Edward to release him.

Guard: (*Disinterested*). We have been instructed not to allow anyone get out even if he is dying.

Around mid-night, Chief Wadelai got a cardiac arrest and passed on. The next morning his body was removed and taken for burial. Immediately, after the burial ceremony, Jonam was initiated as the next Chief. He immediately sought for a meeting with Edward.

Jonam: (*Without greeting*). Mr. Edward or whatever they call you. We are demanding for an immediate release of all our sub-chiefs and kinsmen in your custody. Secondly, all confiscated land must be returned to their respective owners. Thirdly, we must be compensated for the pillage and forced labour.

Edward: Courtesy demands that you greet first. Congratulations, you are now the new chief of this land. I hope you have learned a lesson or two from your father. Unfortunately, your sub-chiefs will only be released if they denounce violence and offer full allegiance to colonial administration.

Jonam: What crime did they commit? You have divided my people. You are turning us against each other. It's true we have put a snake in our hand bag. But, we shall overcome one day.

Edward: Jonam! What are you accusing me off. I have neither divided nor turn your people against each other. The next time you make such baseless accusation. I will have no choice but to lock you up.

Jonam: Edward, you have discretely recruited my kinsmen, including Coope into you ranks to spy and gather intelligence for your illicit motives.

You instructed Coope and his men to confiscate land in Pakwinyo, Ojigo, Pumit, and other areas causing displacement of my people. Many of my kinsmen are incarcerated without trial. Your prisons have turned into labour camps. Do you deny all these. Let me remind you, I am the son of the burning spear. I demand immediate release of my people. I will not ask you again. A lion cannot hide in the grass.

Edward: Ha-ha-ha... are you trying to threaten me? So you are the brave one to tell the lion that his breath smells. What can you do good for nothing son of lioness.

Jonam: When injustice is law then resistance is duty. A bird that flies from the ground onto an anthill does not know that it is still on the ground. If you want to have peace in my land then free my people and seize all hunting, logging and close the forced labour undertakings. I will not warn you again.

He storms out of the meeting while dusting his feet. Jonam is followed by his son Kush and other elders who hard accompanied him. Jonam tasks Kush to mobilize twenty youths. At

73

12:30am the meeting starts

Jonam: What kind of transformation is this that several years later, we are worse off than we were. Our people want their land back. Our people want their labours worth. Our people are demanding for their freedom.

Gathering: Absolutely! We want our land back.

Jonam: Our people were displaced from their land and forced into forced labour undertakings. This is unacceptable and obnoxious. They must return the confiscated land. It's our duty as a generation of leaders and defenders of the burning spear to fulfil this call.

Watmon: I agree with you our chief. A coward should go back to his mothers womb. We must fight. We cannot continue to see our mothers get flogged and humiliated in public. My uncle was hanged to death for failing to deliver on his groundnut quota. This is our land. If we don't brothers, then, we will have nowhere to go but to die here slowly one by one.

Jonam: They hate the idea that we have rights

that must be protected. According to them, we have no rights and our future generations too. But they are wrong. We have rights like any other human race. I am hated for that. There is no crime, I have committed. I have never called for their slaughter or killing under my chieftaincy. I will never call for their slaughter but they must return our land with compensations. I have had that our kinsmen are being killed in the cotton plantations and logging areas. Even, before, I became chief, my nephew was killed because he could not carry an elephant tusk to its final destination. This people are heartless.

Watmon: Chief! A lot of our comrades are living in cramp spaces and makeshift shelters.

Makmot: When the chief speaks, the people listen. We are being denied access to farm land, forests. Our women now cook with dry grass and papyrus. Look at me, I am off age but have no land. You all know how my father was evicted and his land turned into a cotton plantation. Our chief, I am ready to follow your command.

Jonam:	Edward told me in privacy that they are willing to return some of our land but they must be compensated.
Watmon:	Chief, those who are born on top of an anthill take a short time to grow. They are being unreasonable. Did they pay compensation to our fathers and mothers when they evicted them?
Jonam:	Everything has an end. We have to find a solution right now. What should we do to redress this injustice of the big fish?
Kush:	Madness does not govern a community, discussion does. We should approach them for dialogue. They might accept to compensate us.
Makmot:	With due respect to your views. I disagree with your submission. The sheep that wants to grow a long horn must have a strong skull. I suggest we launch an uprising with a series of undertakings.
Kush:	The pot of water falls from your head when you have just reached the door of your house. These people were

welcomed by my late grandfather. They promised to transform our village into a town.

Watmon: Oh! Brother Kush, don't be blind. Can't you see after several decades our lives are worse off. You have travelled at least. Can you compare our progress with the cities you have been too?

Makmot: Our people say that sickness accompanies a waning moon, a new moon cures disease. There is a new leadership dispensation. We are not bound by the decision of Wadelai our fallen chief. Some of you were not even there when they made that bad deal. Where is the agreement? Besides, they have never respected their own word. They killed our chief.

Watmon: If they have any claim, let them furnish us with a copy of the agreement.

Jonam: Well said my comrades. Listen very carefully. You will break into four groups . Each group will comprise of five people. The first group execute uprooting of cotton plantation; group two will uproot ground nut plantation. While group three will burn the logs and group four will burn the ferry so they cannot escape or mobilize reinforcement. Upon execution of your undertaking, use the available canoes to Pawor and other nearby villages. May the God of our forefather protect you all.

Gathering: Long live our chief.

The next morning news of the night destruction reached Edward. He immediately summoned Chief Jonam. Who turned down a meeting request at the fort. However, he was open to a meeting at the cotton plantation.

On the fateful day, Chief Jonam and Mr. Edward begun their meeting with a tour of the cotton plantation to determine the extent of the damage. After a long walk, the two leaders retired under a tree.

Edward: Chief Jonam, you are responsible for these horrible acts. You and your people will pay a heavy price for this. What kind of madness led your youths into burning a ferry. Do you know the cost of a ferry?

Jonam: Edward, is this why you invited me? What is the basis of your accusations. Please provide evidence. I am aware of your sinister motives. You could have orchestrated this acts to justify your impending act. You want to confiscate more land and arrest more youth. It will not work this time.

Edward: I have evidence. You held a meeting

	last night. Didn't you? These damages were conducted under your command.
Jonam:	Furnish me with your evidence or witness testimony. Please don't waste my time. I have better issues that need my urgent attention.
Edward:	Makmot, is in our custody. He has confessed and provided us with all the proceedings of the meeting. Do you still deny having instructed these youth to uproot and burn the ferry?
Jonam:	(*Takes a heavy breathe*). Your actions led my father's death and many of my kinsmen. If you had not jailed my father, he would still be living today.
Edward:	(*Surprised*). The postmortem report is very clear. Your father died from a cardiac arrest. I had no hand in the death of Chief Wadelai.
Jonam:	(*He is shaking and visibly angry. His voice is breaking*). You liar. He strikes Edward on the head and immediately cuts off his head.

He tries to escape from the scene of the

Lord Guy: crime. Edwards guards intercept and arrest him in the middle of the night. Chief Jonam is transferred to Katakenho? face trial.

Jason: On May 10, Chief Jonam lured Mr. Edwards to a cotton plantation and murdered him by beheading him using a hand axe. The state submits that Chief Jonam's act was a pre-meditated murder.

Lord Guy: Does the defense have an opening statement.

Jonam: I have no lawyer. Why are my on trial without a defense lawyer? It's the duty of the authorities to find me a lawyer, in case I am unable to afford a lawyer. This is a miscarriage of justice.

Lord Guy: Chief Jonam, you have been brought before me here in Luzira prison to answer charges of murdering Mr. Edwards. Nevertheless and though you have killed Her Majesty's official. I hope if you cooperate with me, I still may give you a lesser sentence if you can return and calm down your kinsmen who have destroyed several acres of cotton in the field.

Jonam: My lord, I thank you, I submit my petition to the almighty 'Rubanga' the God of my ancestors that he will keep me in this, my honest mind to the last hour that I live… as for the matters you may charge me with I fear from my present weakness that my memory enables me to provide sufficient answers… I should be glad if my blind fold is removed.

Lord Guy: Remove his blind fold. Chief Jonam, did you kill Mr. Edward? If yes, why did you kill him?

Jonam: My Lord, allow me to wear you a bit. As you may be aware, my people were living in 'loka pa lango' the Colonial administration relocated my people across the Nile River into the present day Wadelai village area. The reason provided at that time was that my people would have been extinct by the outbreak of Trypanosomiasis disease caused by tse - tse flies. Whereupon, relocation, my people were subjected to inhuman hard labour in cotton plantation under the command of Mr. Edwards. For several decades, we labored without compensation

When the door opens, the set is in a court room. But for one spot upon which Lapeny standing while holding a notebook. She starts reading…!

The Jonam people once lived across the River Nile in what is today referred to as 'Loka Pa Lango'. They were relocated across the Nile by the Colonial Administrators. The question of land use has been a critical and sensitive political issue in contemporary history of Jonam.

In view of the agrarian nature of the community and the crucial function of rural land as an essential economic resource in this community, it is no – longer astonishing that land use has become a controversial political issue that involves not only opposing observations but also conflict of interests.

Crucially, agriculture continues to be the back born of Jonam's economy. It is the major source of livelihood and income security for approximately ninety - percent of the Jonam's population. Agriculture is a vital source of raw materials for small, medium and large scale industries as well as being the main source of foreign exchange earnings.

The encroachment, exploitation and misuse of the Jonam land has a long history dating back to the colonial era. When the people were forced to grow cotton. Ferry's would dock in Wadlai from Egypt and Sudan to ship cotton wool, elephant and Rhino tusks. The situation has not improved any much. The people continue to suffer from land grabbing and confiscation. Many have lost their lives.

The second Act of the play starts with the trial of Chief Jonam, who ascended to power following the demise of his late father whom many regarded as a sleeping giant. He was accused for tying goats ears on his subjects in order that the colonial wolves would devour them. As a child who slept close to the throne, Jonam, had no respect for cowards because he witnessed widows and orphans being removed from their rightful land. He once told his father that "a sheep spends its whole life fearing wolves but eventually ends up being eaten by a Shepard." He threatened to use his father for sacrifice if he fails to expel Mr. Edward so that he can appease the fallen heroes...!

During the last part of the speech, voices are heard off. Now enters Lord Guy. Who sits on the presiding judges seat. A police siren is heard approaching the court room. The front door is flanked open. Chief Jonam in handcuffs is led by a prison warder into the dock.

Sergeant: (*Rises*), All those with matters in this case step forward and make yourself be heard. Lord Guy is presiding over this case.

Lord Guy:	(*Adjusts his seat and leans forward*). Does the government have an opening statement?
Jason:	On May 10, Chief Jonam lured Mr. Edwards to a cotton plantation and murdered him by beheading him using a hand axe. The state submits that Chief Jonam's act was a pre-meditated murder.
Lord Guy:	Does the defense have an opening statement.
Jonam:	I have no lawyer. Why are my on trial without a defense lawyer? It's the duty of the authorities to find me a lawyer, in case I am unable to afford a lawyer. This is a miscarriage of justice.
Lord Guy:	Chief Jonam, you have been brought before me here in Luzira prison to answer charges of murdering Mr. Edwards. Nevertheless and though you have killed Her Majesty's official. I hope if you cooperate with me, I still may give you a lesser sentence if you can return and calm down your kinsmen who have destroyed several acres of cotton in the field.

Jonam:	My lord, I thank you, I submit my petition to the almighty 'Rubanga' the God of my ancestors that he will keep me in this, my honest mind to the last hour that I live… as for the matters you may charge me with I fear from my present weakness that my memory enables me to provide sufficient answers… I should be glad if my blind fold is removed.
Lord Guy:	Remove his blind fold. Chief Jonam, did you kill Mr. Edward? If yes, why did you kill him?
Jonam:	My Lord, allow me to wear you a bit. As you may be aware, my people were living in 'loka pa lango' the Colonial administration relocated my people across the Nile River into the present day Wadelai village area. The reason provided at that time was that my people would have been extinct by the outbreak of Trypanosomiasis disease caused by tse - tse flies. Whereupon, relocation, my people were subjected to inhuman hard labour in cotton plantation under the command of Mr. Edwards. For several decades, we labored without compensation

whatsoever. It so happen about four market days ago. A few of my kinsmen failed to produce the required quantity of cotton per the specific volume per household. Mr. Edward order their arrest, they fled away. Instead, their wives and children were arrested. Some of the boys and women were hanged at the village square. We have never witnessed this cruelty in the history of the Jonam people. Following this incident, my late father, Chief Wadelai arranged for meeting to follow up on the issue and demands of my people for compensation. Instead, he was arrested together with several chiefs. They were subjected to torture and forced to denounce violence and their demand for compensation. Some of the chiefs who complied were released. My father and two other chiefs remained incarcerated. In the middle of the night my father was pronounced dead. After the death of my father, I assumed the throne. whereupon, I sought to follow up on the pending issues. The next day Mr. Edward labelled a series of accusations against me, including spearheading the uprooting and burning of a ferry. It was these incidents that compelled me to ask Mr. Edward to go with me to visit scene of crime. At the plantation, Mr. Edward told me that I will suffer the fate of my father.

Lord Guy: Jason, do you have the charge?

Jason: Yes, my Lord

Lord Guy: Then, read the charge

Jason: (*Formerly*) that on May 10, you did with motive deny Mr. Edward fundamental human right to life by beheading him in cold blood.

Jonam: How about the boys and women, he ordered to be hanged?

Lord Guy: Did you kill Mr. Edward?

Jonam: Remains silent.

Jason: Silence is admission

Jonam: Silence is no admission and for my silence I am already punished with jail.

Jason: On a charge of death penalty, Lord Guy.

Lord Guy:	For which the punishment is not jail
Jonam:	(*With surprised and shocked*), death comes for us all, my Lord, Yes even you. But, why are there no witness examination?
Jason:	The death of Lord Guy is not in question, Chief Jonam. We do not need witness. Your silence is adequate.
Jonam:	Not even mine, you must prove me guilty of murdering Mr. Edwards.
Lord Guy:	Chief Jonam, do you stand upon you silence to my question inquiring if you killed Mr. Edward?
Jonam:	Yes, I do. I cannot reply without my lawyer.
Jason:	The maxim is "qui tacet consentire" which means silence gives consent. He killed Edward.
Lord Guy:	Chief Jonam, you have been found guilty on the charge of murder. The sentence of the court is that you shall be taken from this court to the execution room and there the machine shall grind you in the presence of your

kinsmen and may God have Mercy on your soul!

Kush: Daddy! Daddy! Daddy! Daddy! Runs towards chief Jonam in the court room and flings himself upon him.

Jonam: Kush, don't trouble yourself. Death comes to us all. My kinsmen present, please defend the Jonam land. One day the long road will come to an end.

Warder: The prison warder disengages Jonam from Kush. Move! haraka! Haraka! Jonam is led to the execution room. He starts a song.... Kush continues to sing as chief Jonam is being consumed bit by bit by the machine...! He starts crying...his relatives brought to witness the execution join him, wuuuh weeeh...maaa...yaaa...!

Kush and Valente are at the train station. They begin an over 600 odd miles between Kampala-Tororo-Mbale-Lira-Gulu and Pakwach. Before embarking on another 40 miles plus on DMC Lorry to Ojigo. Kush enters in the wagon and spots a beautiful lady sitting alone. The train starts to moving...!

Kush: Good morning maiden. Is someone on the seat next to you?

Nakimera: No! You are welcome.

Kush: I am Kush. What is your name? and what is you last destination?

Nakimera: My name is Nakimera. I am travelling to Mbale. How about you?

Kush: Wadelai, a troubled land. Nakimera, I have not slept last night. Allow me to take a nap. Kush dozes off.

Steward: After about three hours, the stewards voice is heard. We are approaching Tororo. Our stop over will last for 20mins. Only those destined for Tororo should disembark. Keep watch of your property...! Twenty minutes pass, the train begins to roll again with loud noise and black smoke. Kush is still sleepy. A voice is heard shouting from outside 'Garr ube wang...gar ube wang...'! Kush wakes up in a haste and throws his bag off the window and arises to exit the train through a locked train door.

Nakimera: Where are you going? Why did you throw your bag?

Kush: Didn't you hear someone shout 'Garr ube wang...'?

Nakimera: What does Garr ube wang mean?

Kush: It means the train is burning.

Nakimera: Ha-ha-ha... That is how thieves in Tororo fleece travelers. I hope you did not have lots of valuables in your bag.

Kush: Nothing much, except my clothing's and shoes and regalia, plus edibles and drinks. How far is the trip to Mbale from Tororo.

Nakimera: Approximately, 50 kilometers.

Kush:	So we will be there in less than two hours.
Nakimera:	Absolutely. Do you work in Wadelai.
Kush:	No! I graduated recently with a degree in literature but no job as yet. What did you study?
Nakimera:	Hmm... I am still in the University, pursuing BA Communication at the University.
Kush:	Fantastic! I wanted to become journalist. When will you graduate?
Nakimera:	(*Pauses as if in search of an answer*). Two years from now.
Kush:	Wish you all the best. Nakimera! Allow me to continue with my nap.
Nakimera:	Oh sure.
	A voice interrupts! Ladies and gentlemen, we are in Mbale. Our stop over will last for 15 minutes...!
Nakimera:	Have a safe trip. It was nice meeting you. I hope our paths will cross again.

Kush:	Bye! Kush folds his jacket and uses it was a pillow. He soon falls asleep for the most part of the journey between Mbale, Lira, Gulu and Pakwach. At 5pm Kush and Valente arrive at Pakwach.
Valente:	Where is your bag?
Kush:	I threw it out of the window in Tororo. After, i heard a man shout 'garr ube wang' as we began our journey from Tororo to Mbale.
Valente:	I wish you sat next to me! Lets go. We will spend a night at Dede (*grandma*) Fasika's home. Tomorrow, we have to catch the lorry at 6am so don't over sleep. Walk fast its getting late. After 20 minutes, Kush and Valente arrive in Puvungu. Kodi...! Eno nga! (*who are you*).
Valente:	It's me Valente and Kush.
Fasika:	Oh, my grandchildren, welcome. Obedi, serve them immediately.
	That night, Kush and Valente were served angara dish with boiled

potatoes. After five minutes, Kush is heard coughing.

Fasika: What is it:

Kush: Coogo omoko idwanda! (*a fish born is stuck in my throat.*)

Fasika: (*Worried*). Wuuuh weeeh, swallow a lump of potato and drink water.

Kush: (*Clears his throat and wipes his tears*). My throat is unblocked. He resumes eating with tears flowing down on his left cheek.

Fasika: Once you are through with your meal, please go have some rest. You have a long journey tomorrow.

Kush: Enters his bed and immediately he falls asleep.

            Late Jonam appears in Kush's sleep ... Kush, don't trouble yourself. Death comes to us all. My kinsmen present, please defend the Jonam land. One day the long road will come to an end.

            Jonam starts singing '... the night seems too long... but day will obviously come. Despite the length of our trouble, it will end one day. There is something mysterious before us. That we might need one day. Let's plant a little fruit tree. So that one day we seat under its shade. Tilt the land my brothers that will protect you from getting hungry in the future. I went to suuq and I saw a beautiful mango I bought it... I went to the riverside and saw a fresh angara and I bought it.. I went to the forest and I saw succulent passion fruit and I harvested it... all this for Jonam...(those are for my Jonam...) I reserve them for Jonam... (those are for my Jonam...) ooyi Jonam, belongs to you... oyiya Jonam, belongs to you... I can testify that Jonam brought peace and love in my life. Mungu has given to Jonam, the secret of life... whenever, there is a problem in the family, Jonam is the one solving them. God has given Jonam than power... there is a tree that has fallen that the birds are worried about. The tree told the birds here are my branches your new home... there is a river that is being covered by water weeds and the fishes are worried... Jonam asks the government to protect the fishes. Jonam told the people to protect the animals and trees... she told farmers to protect the land... this is for Jonam...... I reserve them for Jonam... this is for Jonam... I reserve them for Jonam... this is for Jonam...... I reserve them for Jonam...'

Valente: Kush! Kush! Wake up! wake up! (*while shaking him vigorously*).

Kush: Oh sorry, uncle, what kind of bad luck is this. I was enjoying Dad's song!

Valente: Which Dad? You mean your late father?

Kush: Yes! He was singing for me before you rudely interrupted.

Valente: Oh no! Tipu pa Jonam! Pe iyel latin do...(Spirit of Jonam, don't disturb our son). Kush! Go take you birth and thereafter eat your breakfast. Time is not our best ally. We have a long journey to wadelai. Valente and Kush walk across the street and get aboard a Lorry Truck to Wadelai.

Driver: Jal nyingi nga? Icidu kene? (*Enters the driver*), Comrade! What is your name?

where are you traveling too?

Kush: My name is Kush. Am going to Wadelai (*Kush is lucky sitting next to the driver in a place considered first class. Valente is sitting on sacks and bail of clothes at the rear end of the Lorry*).

Driver: Wadelai, is not at ease. We received the news of the arrest of Chief Jonam and his gruesome execution in Kampala. May his soul Rest in Peace.

Their conversation is interrupted...Just as the driver had taken a sharp corner at speed and he came face to face with another Lorry and a pick up, one attempting to overtake the other. Less than thirty seconds lay between Kush's Lorry and a total smash. The driver swerved the vehicle into the bush on the right and narrowly missed hitting a tree. People were screaming. Kush still could not comprehend what has just happened.

Driver: We are very lucky.

Passenger: Driver, please you are carrying people. Do not be reckless.

Driver:	I leave the matter in God's hands.
Kush:	Let's pray, too many devils on this road.
Driver:	God of our ancestors will protect us. (… for the remaining part of the journey. There was total silence. Exactly 3pm Kush and Valente arrive at Ojigo…).
Kush:	Thank you for bringing us safely home.
Driver:	I hope you enjoyed your journey.
	Kush and Valente, walk for approximately 10 kilometers before arriving at their final destination.

Curtain

Kush: When I speak, people don't accept x 2, they say I am a drunkard and backward, the 'Jonam' were very famous people that all people under the Equatoria province used to respect. You! You! Why are you following me, come, come and we debate about the micro and macro-economic instability of Wadelai. Why are you reversing? Do you know English? If you know English come. The neglect that has lasted for several years has made the Jonam to become very careless. Children all over the villages now move with mucus in their mouth like the nose of turkey. Is this how the Jonam used to live? The white colonialists have been replaced by the black colonialist. These black colonialists continue to confiscate and grab land. This is not acceptable, a few days ago, a fearless son of Jonam was grinded by a machine. Chief Jonam is dead.

Valente :   Starts a song (…toh neko wot ma en acel… toh neko oteka lweny woko…meaning death has robbed me of my only brother…), he is joined by his kinsmen and women weeping.

Coope: Is it Chief Jonam whose life has ended today. Our Chief Jonam has died.

Priest: First keep quite (*dressed in white and holding a Holy Bible*). My people even if we keep on crying Jonam has already died, crying won't help us. Even in the book of 'Yakubu chap 35:1-9', it is written that death is painful and robs us of our dear ones; Jonam death came as a shock. He was grinded by machine like sim - sim 'Muni man cwiny gi col ba!.' (*these whites are heartless*) 'Nen kong twon Jonam gi dwoko ni moko' (*Imagine giant* Jonam *has been reduced into powder*).

Coope: But now my people why don't you even send for me a message? You make Jonam to die without me Coope knowing.

Kush: For me, I have one issue to request, for a long time, Odwel, you have kept us in this village. We are requesting you to help us with a small piece of land to help us burry the body of late Chief Jonam. Piyen muni gi pidu jemi ki gang wa. (*The visitors have planted dangerous items at our home. We cannot burry him there).*

Odwel: (*Moves in front. Looks at the gathering*). I want to tell you people that I have refused your suggestion completely.

Kush: (*Begs him to help*). Please help, how can 6ft x 2ft finish your land).

Odwel: Who does not know that I supported chief Jonam in this village for many years? His land is there. Take his body and burry at his father land.

Kush: We know that but help us, we have nowhere to go. We have been chased from our land.

Coope: Just a small bit cannot spoil our relationship.

Odwel: And you still want I (Odwel) to again burry the body of Jonam. So that tomorrow his spirit asks me for blood? Wek, muni gi yab wang ki kuma? (you want the whites to vent their anger on me?

Coope: How does his spirit ask for blood? This cannot happen.

Help us with just a small piece of land.

Odwel: When a human being dies he/she ceases to be your relative.

Coope: Odwel is it you who is today turning your back for us like a spider does to the sun.

Kush: Odwel remember that every dog has its day. Tomorrow, you will need our support too. The rain does not only fall on one roof.

Odwel: You listen and listen properly. Pick Jonam's remains and burry it where you people know best.

Jacan: My eyes have seen my ears. Where do you want us to take the body? There is no place to bury him. Please assist.

Longoro: My people pick Jonam's remains; I have offered you my land near the Orange tree. My father Odwel transferred his interest over this land to me.

Jacan: Your speech is so good like milk in a calabash. May God bless you abandonly.

Odwel: Longoro, what have you said? You have said that you have got land for burying Jonam? Have you asked me Odwel as your father?

Longoro: Have you now seen how oppression has spoilt our elder who are supposed to lead us? Now they are the ones showing us bad examples. Mzee, you gave me this land long time ago. This land, I now have rights over it. We have to go and burry our fallen chief.

Odwel: You children of nowadays compare yourselves with your fathers. Should any land wrangle occur and you dare come to me, we shall see.

Kush.   Giving just a small piece of land can it, destroy our relationship? Odwel, every fathers dream is to see his son do more than him.

Alonyo: (*Talks to herself*), My time has come, I have to return home today to my ancestral land.

Coope: Alonyo! Alonyo!

Alonyo: Who are you?

Coope: It's me Coope, your uncle.

Alonyo: Today, I want to go home, across the river.

Coope: You cannot manage to go home today, you know our home is still bushy, let me go get people to clear the bushes, you also know that you are blind I have to keep you. When home is cleared I shall come and collect you.

Alonyo: I have said I want to go home and starts to cry and falls on Coope's leg.

Coope: Alonyo, when you cry you make me angrier.

Coope: (*Talks to himself*) Alonyo with her blindness she thinks I will care about her. Just stay in the village with your blindness. In fact the death of your father will bring for me richness and wealth. He laughs............ let me go and sell her father's land. How will she know with her blindness? Your father used to take you to the toilet, now I can't do that. I want to assure you stop coiling yourself around my leg like a tick attaches itself on a cow's udder. I did not kill your father, it's not me. I will have to grow rich if I don't then I will never grow rich. Even if with witchcraft I have to grow rich.

Coope   This land belong to our late chief Jonam but he is dead and I am in charge now.

Jacan   How much is it?

Coope: Two hundred millions Uganda shillings.

Jacan: Two hundred million! Are you selling a human being?

Coope: My brother, if you don't have two hundred million shillings, you can take you leave.

Jacan: Coope, I am ready to pay you one hundred million cash.

Coope: This land has petroleum deposits underneath. It seems you are shortsighted investor.

Jacan: Petroleum deposits. How did you know?

Coope: Remember, I used to work at the fort. They never built a fort here just to hunt only. Anyway, since you are not interested, let me look for another buyer.

Jacan: Hear is your 200,000,000/=

Coope: uuuh eeeh...ha-ha-ha and falls on the ground in happiness and jubilation. Starts a song ... Omera dwe taar...nyamera wacidu Iroma...x2

Coope: At this rate, I will be a billionaire. Toolit, died before Jonam but Celina is still stuck on that land without shame. This widow wants to benefit from government compensation. I have heard that government is licensing land into blocks for petroleum oil exploration. Land owners will be compensated handsomely. My late brothers land is in a strategic location. If I don't kick Celina and her children, I will miss out. A tse - tse that rests on the scrotum must get a five star slap. Let me phone Krishna and seal the deal.

Coope: (*He meets with Krishna*). Hello, Krishna. I understand you are in search of prime land for rice growing. Are you still interested.

Krishna: Absolutely, have you found a seller?

Coope: Yes, I have land in a prime location and very close to the river.

Krishna: Lets meet on second market day. So that I can have a look and explore possibilities of buying.

Coope: See you soon.

Krishna: Bye!

Coope: Wow! Another raw deal. Let me go retrace the land boundaries in readiness for our meeting with Krishna.

Celina: Coope, why are you sweating like a Christmas goat. What brings you to my land this morning?

Coope: 'Mon yamu tiye ki twero ikum ongom?' (*Since when did women attain rights to own customary land?*).

Anyango: Coope, why are you sweating like you escape from a crocodiles jaws?

Coope: Don't you know the distance between Mutir village and Pakwinyo village?

Atuku: Mama, haven't you heard that Satan has bought land in Ojigo. People were saying that Satan has registered his dissatisfaction with people like Coope. He said that he has no space for people like Coope in hell. He wants to sort them out on earth. Coope sweating is a clear indication that he has begun his sentence. He is suffering from the cat mentality that all rats belong to them. In this connection, Coope, believes that all land belongs to him.

Coope: I am not a Catholic like you and your mother who believes in hell. Who told you rich men will go to hell.

Anyango: Mum, poverty is a lion. No one will help you to fight it when it attacks you. Forget Coope, lets continue to plant our seeds.

Atuku: Coope, remember a forest cannot stop existing if a tree is cut. The demise of our father is not the end of the World. We shall overcome sinister people like you.

Coope:	(*Hmmm...*) I know the children of darkness hunt like wolves. They can devour you if you are alone. Who is singing...!
Kush:	Enters with a song '... kongi pe...kongi pe...anyira catholic... kongi pe... doo... anyira Silam mwodo wag i gweno...'
Coope:	Kush, in a 'ye lacuwo ki kume' (*Kush, you're the man*)
Kush:	Coope, why are you here on a widows land, this early?
Coope:	Kush, come, I have good news for you. Do you know that my late brother was not a serious man.
Kush:	Who? You mean late Toolit?
Coope:	Yes, Toolit!
Kush:	What was wrong with him? I knew him as a very hard working and responsible man.
Coope:	How could Toolit, succumb to death and leave such yellow woman like

	Muyembe (ripe mango)? If it was me, I would have given death a good run for his money.
Kush:	Coope, death does not ask for permission. It comes and surprises everyone. It takes you unaware.
Coope:	You are right! Let's discuss how we will share the eating's.
Kush:	Which eating's? Remember, the evils that men do will go with them and the good deeds will remain with his people.
Coope:	You take Celina and I take the land. What is your opinion?
Kush:	Coope, dogs do not run together with cats. I cannot be party to your heartless proposal. I don't want to provoke the wrath of the oracle (*Abila pa kwaro*) on me.
Celina:	Coope, I have been listening to your conversation.
Coope:	Pulls his belt and starts flogging Celina and her children.

He chases Celina and her children. Unfortunately, youngest boy jumps into the river in an attempt to swim across and drowns.

Coope: Kush, you are still following me.

Kush: Where is the young boy?

Coope: He is lucky. He jumped in the river and swum away.

Kush: Coope, you are a disgrace. Tradition, dictates that you as the eldest remaining brother of the late, should have been the one to take care of Celina and her children. This white people's culture has ruined you.

Coope: Kush, if you don't leave in the count of three. I will flog you too.

Kush: Let me go but the clan leaders must here this. Two wrongs don't make a right.

Coope: There is no need to cry crocodile tears, they invited it, they should live with it.

Coope: I can hear a vehicle approaching my

location. I hope its Krishna? This deal must be concluded today. The vehicle stops. Krishna disembarks.

Coope: Welcome! Krishna. You journey was like waiting for Christmas.

Krishna: My apologies, I had a vehicle tyre puncture. It took me longer than normal to replace the tyre.

Coope: I understand. So this is the land, I informed you about in our last meeting.

Krishna: what is the size of the land?

Coope: As I communicated earlier, this land is 200 acres. Do you want us to reach every corner of the land.

Krishna: No – no - no! just show me the key features that mark the boundaries.

Coope: Excellent! Can you see that huge Mvule tree over there?

Krishna: Yes!

Coope: From the Mvule, follow a straight line to that other mahogany tree on the slop of the hill, then to the river bank and then back to the road.

Krishna: How much is cost of an acre of the land?

Coope: Only two (2) million Uganda shillings

Krishna: That's too much. I am offering 500,000 Uganda shillings per acre.

Coope: No - no - no, this land is flat as you can see and ready for mechanized agriculture, including irrigation. Rice grows here quite well.

Krishna: In that case, lets meet in middle, one (1) million Uganda shillings.

Coope: Let me assist you as brother.

Krishna: Do we have a deal?

Coope: Yes!

Krishna: Where is the title?

Coope: My brother, if you want this land then don't ask me for the title. I already told you this is my property.

Krishna: What if tomorrow someone claims the same piece of land? I undertook some consultation and was informed that this land belonged to your late brother's wife, Ms. Celina.

Coope: Celina, was born in loka pa lango. It was the colonial administration that in around 1890s moved the likes of Celina's parents across the River Nile to save them from Trypanosomiasis as we are have been told. She has a legitimate claim in loka pa lango, not here.

Krishna: I am satisfied with your submission. Here is 100 million Uganda shillings.

Coope: Wooo hooo! Starts a song....okello wiye ki kampala awobe...huuuh... gini kume ngwee motara....okello wiye ki kin lum...x3 wang ma dong a wilo plot ki kampala (*I must buy a plot in Kampala*).

Kush: Coope, manaka ndii akandere ikin lum. Awinju lok wu weng (*Coope, I have been hiding in the bush and have heard all your conversations and exchanges*). Why are you moving

115

backwards. Its only witches who move backwards.

Coope: Kush, it's you who is a native doctor. Nothing escapes you in this village. What do you want? Okay, have five (5) millions shillings and go integrate with your mates.

Kush: I don't need your dirty money. I heard you tell Krishna that some Jonam people, including Celina's parents used to live ki loka pa lango. That is true, but let me inform you. The Jonam people who have attempted to access their ancestral land ki loka pa lango have been killed in cold blood. To date, the perpetrators are living at large. Where do you want Celina and our children to go?

Coope: Not all chimpanzees that enter a maize plantation come out satisfied. Since you have claimed that they are your children, then, take Celina and her children to your house.

Kush: You operate like a python. You malign people. But, someday the long arm of the law will catch up with you.

Coope: But, you also know that sometimes, if
           you want to catch a wolf you need to
           tie a bait to a tree.

Kush: I have now confirmed that one cannot
           not nominate a hyena to preside in a
           gathering discussing how goats are to
           be kept. Let me go and report the
           matter to our elders.

ACT THREE

The scene is as for start of Act two. When the curtain rises the state is in dawn. Save for the spot, in which Lapeny stands. She carries a bottle, a place marked by hand and wears cap.

Lapeny: the scene starts in the second planting season, several months after Coope has displaced widows, boys, girls by selling his late brothers land. By this time a lot of water has flown under the bridge.

Lights rise to show Jacan's children standing in their garden. Exit Lapeny. Enters Jacan dressed in black short and white t-shirt. He walks up and down sowing seeds and is watched by his children and wife.

Jacan	(*Is in the garden with his daughter and son, he start a song*) "ma ana bulu weeh lutwa gina ngo man abino dongo lobo yah...........................fuur mit bulu" he is sowing seeds?
Kush:	(*Staggering with a goad in his hands*). But you! You! Am talking to you, you! What kind of relationship is there between you and the people of the late

Toolit? It means you people only help those who are blind only. How about us drunkards, where do you put us.

Jacan: *(Politely shoves Kush)*. You are stepping on my seeds. Please do not invite my anger. You have left the main road and preferred to trespass through my garden please leave this place.

Kush: Let me tell you, you have taken me as a drunkard but an elder once said that "everything has a beginning and an end"

Jacan: Kush, let me tell you, I have just bought this land and I want to gain something from this land . Please go away.

Kush: Am going but you wait! Wait! Wait!

Jacan: My God? This man who has been spoilt by alcohol. He even studied and graduated from the University, his parents wasted there sleep claiming to be looking for a child.

He start a song to motivate him to dig.....................

Jacan:	Some people are singing in their garden like I am doing. But that song is different from mine.
Jacan:	Let me continue with digging.
Odwel:	Do you think that, "warm water can be cooled with warm water?"
Otim:	'A coward should go back to his mothers' stomach.'
Kush:	Starts a song..........................Wan dong laro ongom ki tong ......ongom kwaro waa'
Jacan:	Eeeeeh, it seems there is now some difference in that song.
Otim.	Jacan. Who has given you the authority to dig on this land?
Odwel:	Who has given you the authority to plough here?
Jacan:	Why do you people come to me as if I am a wrong killer? I have bought this land from Coope.
Otim:	Which Coope?

Jacan:	Coope, the son of Obongotik ngec. Where is he?
Jacan:	He is at his place. Get up and take us there.
Otim:	Let me go and get him: What if we find out that he has not sold the land to you? (They continue with the song about traditional customary land..........................)
Otim:	Ber-iwu! why are you talking to yourself. What is the problem?
Ber-iwu:	There is a problem.
Otim	What is it?
Ber-iwu:	Coope, the son of Obongotik ngec sold late Toolit's land to Jacan and now they are all gathered at my place.
Otim:	All these problems for you?
Ber-iwu:	In fact you as Otim as Local Council two (2). I was planning to come to invite you for tomorrow's meeting at my place.

Kush: Can I join you?

Ber-iwu: All of them are rats in the same house.
             You also come tomorrow.

Otim: Kush, tomorrow, we have a meeting at
             Ber-iwu's place. About your friend
             Coope.

Kush: Coope?

Otim: He has sold late Toolit's land. The
             meeting will start at 10:00am

Kush: Let's go, I will abuse him and his
             mother in English. He thinks, he is
             clever.

Otim: He will punch you. Ha-ha-ah...

Kush: Let's go. A donkey which goes to grow
             horns returns with its ears cut off.

Ber-iwu: Where have these people gone?

Ber-iwu: Even if the Jonam people don't keep
             time, there are others who do, lets
             organize this place.
             (*People begin to enter and take their sits,*

one member, Jonam's, even if he or she has a watch on his or her wrist he or she does not keep time).

Ber-iwu: The weather looks cloudy. I want us to start the meeting but the person who has made us to gather here isn't there?

Otim: Kush, knows where his friend is?

Kush: Coope is drinking at Aparoku's place, I will not tell you people.

Odwel He has already said it.

Otim: I am an authority; I will go and get him.

Jacan: Even if he is not there, I have this to submit, we should really warn him today, selling land it's him, fighting its him, please he should be warned.

Otim: Here is Coope.

Jacan: My name is Jacan Tango.

Kush: What did you say your name is?

Tango: My name is Jacan Tango.

Kush:	These are the people buying land in Loka pa lango. We don't have the names like Tango in Jonam.
Tango:	Don't interrupt me with your stupid talks. It cannot be past five months ago when, Coope came to me that he is selling land, and I got money and gave him. To my surprise he had sold me the land of some blind lady.
Otim	Isn't that Alonyo's land? I think it is.
Alonyo:	Coope you told me that you are going to organize home then you will come and take me. Wuwe...haaa...eeeh. (*She starts crying*).
Tango:	I have now reminded Alonyo of other problems yet her only problem used to be her blindness. I now want to summarize in this way. Her people came and chased me. I want my money to be given back.
Otim:	I want to ask Tango.
Ber-iwu	Ask.
Otim:	You said you have bought the land, where is the letter that shows that you

have bought? The law of this government states that you should have a title as an evidence of transaction. Show us so that we finish this issue.

Kush: Documentation. Let him furnish us with the original land title.

Tango: Coope, deceived me that this matter does not need any witness. There was no witness, and no title. My elders your appearance is making me afraid.

Kush: You people think I am a drunkard. Who can answer me, do you think that if an anthill is left to one termite, can it build it.

Tango: We have been thinking that he is a drunkard, yet he has sense.

Kush: Keep quiet, other people say that if you want to kill anthill, you have to clear the top flat. Do you think by that you would have killed an anthill?

Nimungu: Yes, you would have killed the anthill.

Gathering: Nooo....!

Kush:	If you want to kill the anthill you have to dig deep to the roots and remove the queen that is when you will say that you have killed the anthill but not just clearing the top. Let me tell you. The anthill is the beginning of civilization in Jonam land.
Gathering:	You have started speaking in English.
Kush:	Tell me what has brought all the fighting like that of Coope. But Coope is good. He has made my life simple. Everywhere I go Kush, everywhere Kush.
	Anyhow, Coope has committed a very big crime, you all fear to tell him his problem. Let me say it today. He chased his wife, if you see her big bums. If Coope hated his wife, he should have given her to me.
Ber-iwu:	Now Kush, sit down. You have heard what has been relayed by Kush.
Kush:	(*Interjects*) Coope is holding land in trust for the family members.
Otim:	Let me talk

Kush:	Let me say something. You Local Councilors (LC's) always when you want to speak you want money, today, you are going to talk for free.
Otim:	That is Kush's issues. Today, this matter is not before me. I don't want to waste time. I will go straight to Jacan's issue. Some minutes ago, I asked Tango to produce for us his letter. You said that there is no letter. I will tell you openly that you have no right of that land and the right of that land falls back to Alonyo.
Kush:	That is a gone case.
Ber-iwu:	I wish to thank all elders who have given their views. I also want to thank our Local Council Two (LC2) for the role he has played. I have got up to summarize this meeting, but before I do so I want to take you back to what Kush has been saying. Kush has been speaking in tongues.
Kush:	Narrate to them so that they can understand. They call me a drunkard.
Ber-iwu:	He rapped that the anthill is the beginning of civilization in Jonam

	land. How do you translate that? Let me ask. If you dig the anthill what do you find?
Members:	You get white ants, termites and the queen.
Ber-iwu:	I want all of you to stay with open ears. Is there a day that you find a termite goes to bite the queen?
Members:	Nooo............. Not at all
Ber-iwu:	Why are we Jonam's killing ourselves? Jonam's used to unite like the termites who have built that strong anthill you are seeing there.
Kush:	If I had not spoken would you have known.
Ber-iwu:	Let me ask you again. What is the colour of the anthill?
Member:	It is red.
Ber-iwu:	Kush, also made mentioned that Jonam's suffering for so many years has made the anthill to cry with blood. How does this affect us? I want to ask. Who has not suffered in this land?

Members.	Every one.
Ber-iwu.	Jonam's blood has been shed for so many years and that can be seen from the colour of the river. Our problem has entered deep like the queen of the anthill. Like Kush said you cannot just clear the surface and think you have killed the anthill. You have to dig deep so as to remove the anthill. Therefore, if we want to remove the problems in Jonam, we have to dig deep to remove the root causes of the problem so that Jonam's remain respected as it was before. For this reason, I want to remind you that we have to unite like the termite so that we can be strong like before.
	I understand that now days there are very many land wrangles, tomorrow I want us to plant trees on our boundary to stop this land wrangles in future. What type of trees should we plant?
Member:	Eucalyptus, orange, Nsambya, Carcia.
Kush:	We plant cassava to help in brewing 'guli' (*alcohol*....)

Ber-iwu:	Those types of trees like carcia, eucalyptus are the ones to be planted while your children are seeing, so that tomorrow your children will remember that our parents last time planted a tree to mark our land boundary. To stop this kind of wrangling like that of Coope. For this, I will meet with elders from loka pa lango to discuss this with them on this issue.

One other thing, I have heard that the youth are killed in loka pa lango. This land wrangles needs to be resolved as soon as possible. We have many vulnerable people like the blind, widows, orphans, sick, crippled and those who have been displaced as a result of land wrangles. We should support all of them and stop this killings. Have you heard me? |
Members:	Yes.
Ber-iwu:	Now to summarize Coope get up and start asking for forgiveness from all you have wronged one at a time.
Alonyo:	Start with me.

Kush: Coope's offenses are equivalent to
            murder. He should be subject to 'Mato
            oput' so that he is totally cleansed and
            reconciled with the community.

Nimungu: According to our restorative justice
            system. There is no provision for
            imprisonment or death penalty for an
            offender. The main reason was
            because our ancestors valued the
            sanctity of human life and preserve it
            and that is why there is no
            imprisonment and death penalty.

Aparoku: The perpetrators must be
            rehabilitated into the society through
            these processes. We do not believe in
            death penalty and we don't believe in
            imprisonment.

Ber-iwu: We have to reconcile and rehabilitate
            Coope into the society because of the
            value we attach to the sanctity of
            human life and we must preserve it.

Kush: But, he has to drink the bitter root of
            the Mato Oput tree.

Otim: Chief should watch over the
            negotiation between the two families.

Aparoku: We must negotiate so that he can pay
               blood feud for Towili who drown in
               the river.

Ber-iwu: Aparoku, you have spoken well. Our
               ancestors provided for payment of
               blood feud.

Nimungu: In our tradition the compensation for
               murder is provided for.

Otim: He was to bring fifty Cows and seven
               goats, plus two sacks of 'moko'.

Nimungu: He has to pay blood feud before we
               begin with mato oput.

Aparoku: Payment of blood feud will stop any
               act of revenge. Without payment of
               blood feud more deaths will follow.

Coope: I have brought the fifty cows and
               seven goats and two sacks of moko.

Kush: Now that payment of blood feud has
               been completed let us begin the
               process of mato oput.

Ber-Iwu: Have the two families brought the two
               animals.

Otim:	Yes, here are the two animals. Celina brought a he goat and Coope brought a Ram.
Ber-Iwu:	How about the crashed oput tree root?
Nimungu:	All requirements are here.
Ber-iwu:	Coope and Celina come in front and kneel facing each other.
Kush:	Coope must tell us the truth and accepts his guilt and repent.
Otim:	Yes, this will symbolize the end to bitterness between the two families.
Aparoku:	Absolutely, this mato oput will lead to healing and reconciliation.
Ber-Iwu:	What is cardinal and paramount is that Coope must accept that he did it.
Kush:	Coope, did your actions lead to the death of Towili?
Coope:	Yes, my actions led to the death of the young boy.
Ber-iwu:	Now, confess and seek for forgiveness.

Coope: Thank you my clan members for giving me such a wonderful lesson. I have learnt and will change; I want to tell all of you that alcohol made me go astray. I have stopped drinking alcohol today.

Tango: If you regret then its good.

Coope: First, I want to apologize to Tango. Alcohol made me commit this evil. Secondly, i know if a disabled person get annoyed with you it can cause problems to someone. Alonyo, your land has been given back to you that is ok. Tomorrow I will buy items from the market and bring for you.

Ber-Iwu: Now, the two families do accept and take over the responsibilities?

Families: Yes, we take full responsibility that our son Coope committed the heinous crime.

Ber-Iwu: Okay, lay the two sheep close to each other facing opposite directions. Cut them into two equal halves and share between the two families. Take some of blood and mix with oput in the calabash.

Gathering: Let them drink it. Starting with Coope then Celina so that they cleanse themselves.

Coope: (*Picks the calabash and sips the oput mixture*). Haaa.... It's too bitter.

Gathering: Swallow, swallow, swallow. Ah now you are liberated from your sin.

Ber-Iwu: Celina, bend with your hands behind your back like Coope did and drink the oput in the calabash.

Kush: (Hugs Coope). Now you are a clean man. Come let's dance and celebrate your renewal.

Members: Start singing........................END

OCHANDA Walter: A Biographical Note

Walter Ochanda was born in 1982 in the village of Wadelai in North Western Uganda. After studying international development, Mediation, peace and security and law at the University of Bath, University of Addis Ababa, University of South Wales and University of Nairobi, he went to work for Intergovernmental and International organization in Djibouti, Eritrea, Ethiopia, Kenya, Somalia, South Sudan and Sudan. The Trials of Jonam, his first play was published in 2020. It has sold hundred copies and has been translated in few languages.

Ochanda has also written several articles and journals. Uganda becoming a secretly watched state and agricultural trade liberalization. A collection of essays and policy analysis was published in 2016.

Ochanda has lectured and held public lectures in Universities and colleges. Among the many honours he has received are the University of Bath outstanding scholars award 2011 and Commonwealth scholar award for outstanding academic records.

Ochanda now lives in Kampala, Uganda and works at Addis Ababa, Ethiopia. He is married and has two children.

THE TRIALS

OF

JONAM

Printed in Great Britain
by Amazon

47436480R10086